Better Homes and Gardens®

THE NEW

father

BOOK

By Wade F. Horn, Ph.D., and Jeffrey Rosenberg, M.S.W.,
of the National Fatherhood Initiative

Better Homes and Gardens® Books
Des Moines, Iowa

Better Homes and Gardens® Books
An imprint of Meredith® Books

New Father Book
Authors: Wade F. Horn, Ph.D., and Jeffrey Rosenberg, M.S.W.
Project Development Editor: Christopher Cavanaugh
Associate Art Director: Lynda Haupert
Copy Chief: Angela K. Renkoski
Contributing Copy Editor: Becky Danley
Electronic Production Coordinator: Paula Forest
Editorial and Design Assistants: Judy Bailey, Susan McBroom, Jennifer Norris, Karen Schirm, Barbara Suk
Production Director: Douglas M. Johnston
Production Manager: Pam Kvitne
Assistant Prepress Manager: Marjorie J. Schenkelberg

Meredith® Books
Editor in Chief: James D. Blume
Design Director: Matt Strelecki
Managing Editor: Gregory H. Kayko
Executive Health Editor: Alice Feinstein

Director, Sales & Marketing, Retail: Michael A. Peterson
Director, Sales & Marketing, Special Markets: Rita McMullen
Director, Sales & Marketing, Home & Garden Center Channel: Ray Wolf
Director, Operations: Valerie Wiese

Vice President, General Manager: Jamie L. Martin

Better Homes and Gardens® Magazine
Editor in Chief: Jean LemMon

Meredith Publishing Group
President, Publishing Group: Christopher M. Little
Vice President, Consumer Marketing & Development: Hal Oringer

Meredith Corporation
Chairman and and Chief Executive Officer: William T. Kerr

Chairman of the Executive Committee: E.T. Meredith III

Cover photograph: Tom Upton

All of us at Better Homes and Gardens® Books are dedicated to providing you with the information and ideas you need to stay healthy. We welcome your comments and suggestions about this book. Write to us at: Better Homes and Gardens Books, Health Editorial Department, RW–206, 1716 Locust St., Des Moines, IA 50309–3023.

Notice to Readers: This book is intended to provide you with information about health and child care. It is not intended to be a medical guide or to serve as a substitute for advice from your doctor. Every adult's health needs are unique. Every child's health care needs are unique. Diagnosis and treatment must be done through a health care professional. Please consult with your doctor for all your health care needs.

Contents

the call to be a
good father

We know that, because you're reading this book, we have something important in common with you: You are committed to being a good father to your children. Of course, being a good dad takes more than commitment. It takes knowledge, patience, understanding, and skills. Where does a man go to learn how to be a good dad?

For most of us, our first and best teacher is our own dad. But no matter how terrific our own dad may have been, there are some things we would like to do differently when we become dads ourselves. And, unfortunately, some men grow up with dysfunctional dads, and some even with no dad at all.

One place men can look to find out what it means to be a good dad is the popular culture—places like television, music, and movies. But far too often dads are portrayed in these places as bumbling buffoons or worse. All too rarely is fatherhood portrayed either realistically or skillfully in the popular culture.

Another place men can look to learn about being a good dad is books. There are, in fact, numerous books written about how to be a good parent. Unfortunately, most of these are written by or for women. Nothing wrong with that, of course; mothers are parents, too. But men do bring entirely different qualities and inclinations to the parenting equation. Good fathers are not simply good mothers in trousers.

That's why we wrote this book. We wanted to help men embarking upon the fatherhood journey get a bit of an inside peek at what they are getting themselves into—the challenges and the joys—and to offer some commonsense advice without a lot of psychobabble. In fact, you won't learn much about psychology giants Sigmund Freud and Jean Piaget in this book. You will learn a good number of practical tips from dads who learned the hard way. That's who we are.

Throughout this book, we refer to "we" quite often. We share a number of anecdotes about our own families to illustrate points we make. We aren't just advocates for fathers; we're fathers ourselves, walking the walk on a daily basis. To help give these stories some context, we'd like to introduce ourselves to you individually.

Wade Horn, Dad

As a clinical child psychologist, I have had a number of jobs: professor at a Big Ten university, director of outpatient psychological services at an inner-city hospital, practitioner in private practice, presidential appointee to head an agency in the federal government, member of two national commissions focusing on children's issues, and executive director of a children's advocacy organization. My own father says that this varied career reflects my inability to hold a job; I like to think otherwise.

Somewhere along the line, I can't remember exactly when, it occurred to me that what was causing so many children to be in need of so many services was the absence in their lives of an involved, committed, and responsible father. For some children, their father was physically absent. For others, their father was physically present, but nonetheless psychologically absent. Either way, the result was often the same: depressed, angry, and troubled kids. I was determined to do something about it. In effect, I was tired of pulling kids out of the river, so I resolved to walk upstream and try to stop them from being pushed in.

Along the way, I discovered something about myself. I, too, have, at times at least, been an absent dad. At the moment of my first daughter's birth, like many fathers, I promised her that I would love her forever and always, and quietly spoke of all the things she and I would do together. Two years later, I made the same promise and the same plans at the birth of my second daughter.

But, like many dads, I got busy. Busy with career and making money. Busy with buying a home and filling it with things. Busy with the everyday routine of life. Although my love for my two daughters never wavered, my attention sometimes did. "Forever and always" all too frequently came to mean "tomorrow."

Then, at age 34, I was diagnosed with cancer.

As I lay recuperating from cancer surgery, I thought a lot about my life—about my successes and failures, my accomplishments and regrets. It was then that my earlier promises came back to me. I realized that if I were to die, what I would miss most was not my career, or my money, or the things I had worked so hard to acquire. No, if I were to die,

what I would miss most would be those two little girls who, each morning before going to school, quietly came into the bedroom to give their sick daddy a kiss.

I vowed that whatever happened with my illness, I would spend whatever time I had left paying better attention to my promises of *"forever and always."* I vowed that I would slow down a bit and enjoy the journey more.

My hope in writing this book is that it will help new dads fulfill their own promises of forever and always to their children, so they won't have to face a life-threatening illness before they realize that the most important job they will ever have is to be found not in the workplace but in the home.

Of course, I am not a perfect dad; just ask either of my teenage daughters. I've certainly made my share of mistakes. But I like to think I've learned a thing or two along the way as well. My hope is that you'll find this book of help to you as you embark upon your own journey, make your own mistakes, and find your own joys.

Wade F. Horn, Ph.D.
President, The National Fatherhood Initiative
Father of Christen and Caroline

Jeff Rosenberg, Dad

In real life, many of my dreams came true when my wife and I were blessed with our three kids. Creating this book gives me the opportunity to write about the most important part of my life: being a dad. While I've occasionally stumbled, I've also learned a lot. The relationships I've built with my three children always bring me great joy, which means I'm doing something right.

I coach baseball, I often take the kids on day trips by myself (relieving my wife of the stress of raising twins!), I go to lots of cartoon movies. In fact, most of the fun I have somehow involves my children.

Suffice it to say, I've worked hard at being a dad, and it's hard work I love. My wife, Pat, and I have set the world record for continuous exhaustion—remember we have two terrible two-year-olds. Wait until you have one (or maybe two!) and you'll see what I'm talking about. But I've also developed the sure-fire cure for parental exhaustion:

Me: "Mylene, how much does Daddy love you?"

Mylene: (spreading her arms as wide as they will go) "Too much!"

Me: "Justin, how much does Daddy love you?"

Justin: (also spreading his arms wide) "Too much!"

Then the three of us hug, which is usually brought to a crashing end when 8-year-old Jeremy jumps on top of the hugging mass.

Hopefully, the advice that my coauthor and I offer can help you build an equally fulfilling relationship with your children.

I know I learned a lot just by writing this book and working closely with my coauthor, Wade Horn, a clinical psychologist who dispenses commonsense advice. In fact, I've applied some of the advice about building a strong marriage to my own marriage. Living in a house with 2-year-old twins combined with the fact that my wife and I each run our own small business is, to say the least, taxing on a marriage.

I followed Wade's advice about how to work on your partnership with your wife and avoiding the 50-percent trap (you'll just have to read the book to see what I'm talking about). Now I love my wife more than ever, and she can tolerate me better than ever.

There's a lot of good advice in this book. I use it myself, and so does Wade. I hope that you find this book helpful. And I hope that you find the same joy in fatherhood that I have.

Jeff Rosenberg
Father of Jeremy, Mylene, and Justin

it takes a man to be a dad

You're wondering:

What makes a good dad?

Will I be a good dad?

Am I a good dad?

Tough questions.

Many men think the answers to these questions are found in the workplace. They leave home early every morning, barely seeing their children, and come home late at night after a long day at work. Exhausted, they grab something quick to eat and collapse on the couch. The only thing that makes them feel good about this lifestyle is believing that going to work and bringing home a paycheck is what makes a man a good father.

Sam Marcsisak and son Samuel, 1996

If you ask kids what makes a good dad, their answers have little, if anything, to do with Dad's paycheck. They use different words, but the children's answers are the same: love, time, commitment, and responsibility. Certainly, bringing home a paycheck can be an important part of being a good father. But to our kids, the most important thing good dads invest in is not stocks, bonds, or mutual funds, but them.

Bill Brett with daughter Eily Ann, and son Joe, 1996

Love

If you're looking for the right stuff to be a good father, look in your heart. It's right there: a deep, enduring, and basically irrational love. This is not a love that says, "As long as I am happy being a father, you can count on me." This is a love that says, "I am here for you always, through thick and thin, whether you please me or not."

It's the kind of love that says to your child, "When you go to sleep at night, you can count on me to protect you from danger. If the house catches on fire or burglars break into the home, I will risk my own life to save you. When you are playing outside and, God forbid, you accidentally run into the street in front of a speeding car, I will throw myself into its path to save your life."

A father's love for his children makes him brave, determined, and protective. It's the closest most men will ever get to feeling like John Wayne in *The Green Beret*, Kevin Costner in *The Untouchables*, or Wesley Snipes in *Passenger 57*, or, well, you get the drift. When you tuck your child into bed at night, you know—just know, to the depths of your being—that you would lay down your life to protect that child. That's the purest feeling of what it is to be a man that most of us will ever have a chance to experience.

We're not saying that loving your children is always easy. Children can be difficult. They are often demanding, self-centered, pouty, messy, and dirty. There are times when our children drive us up the wall, like when the VCR will no longer accept tapes, and you know it's the work of little hands. But still, we love them dearly.

The big question is, how best to show your children how much you love them? For many years, there has been an unfortunate myth that fathers should not show any kind of physical affection to their children.

Some fathers still believe that hugging their sons will cause them to become sissies. Some dads worry so much about this, that they even avoid giving their young sons a goodnight kiss. Strong, distant, macho men: This is the view these men have of what it takes to be a good father to their sons. They're wrong.

The truth is, boys who get lots of physical affection from their fathers grow up with a healthier and more secure sense of their own masculinity than boys whose fathers do not display affection easily. So if you want your son to grow up to be a secure man, make sure you hug him a lot when he's young.

If you have a daughter, she, too, needs your hugs and kisses. The first relationship your daughter will ever have with a man is with you.

If she loves and feels loved by you, she'll grow up feeling worthy and deserving of love. When she is older and begins dating, she will likely seek out boyfriends who show the same kind of love she received from you, her father.

If you are supportive, kind, and affectionate when your daughter is young, she will seek out boyfriends who are like you—supportive, kind, and affectionate.

But, if you're distant, cold, and aloof when she's young, she will seek out boyfriends who are also distant, cold, and aloof. It's not an exaggeration to say that your daughter's future dating and even marital happiness depends in great measure upon how you treat her when she is a child.

Look at it this way: Peek into the future and imagine when your daughter is 17. Do you want a nice young man who dresses decently showing up at the door to take her to the movies or an impertinent kid with a pierced nose who calls you Pops? So, quick, go give your daughter a hug and kiss before it's too late.

But loving one's children is not enough. A good father also must love the mother of his children. Numerous studies over the years have shown that children whose parents love, respect, and support each other do better in school, have higher self-confidence, and are less likely to have emotional or behavioral problems. They are also healthier than

15 ways to show fatherly love

1. A kiss
2. A hug
3. A knowing wink
4. A "high-five"
5. A "thumbs up"
6. Roughhousing on the floor (or anywhere else)
7. A piggyback ride
8. Cuddling on the couch
9. Giving advice
10. Asking for your child's advice
11. Listening to your child
12. Tucking your child in bed and saying goodnight
13. Giving your child a special nickname
14. Calling your child from work just to say "hi"
15. Saying "I love you"—a lot!

children whose parents do not love, respect, and support each other.

For example, a recent study of students in sixth through eighth grades published in the scientific journal *Adolescence* found that children's self-image was dependent on how loving the children's fathers were toward their wives.

So while you are working on being a good dad, it is at least equally important that you work at being a good husband. This means being supportive and loving toward your wife and making sure you and your wife have time to be alone together. It also means realizing that a lifetime together requires having the strength to work through tough times.

OK, let's get real here for a minute. We know that many (way too many) marriages these days end in divorce. If you're a single dad or a stepdad who's picked this book up hoping it will help you be a better father, congratulations. This book is filled with tips and skills that will help you be a good father even from a distance, even if the children are not your biological children. In fact, Chapter 7 deals entirely with the problems unique to single fathers and to stepdads.

What about those studies that say that a loving relationship between a child's parents helps children do better in school and helps protect the chil-

---

When it comes to love, here's our rule of thumb. It is simply impossible to say "I love you" or to hug your children too much. Of course, giving lots of hugs and kisses will be easy at first—all of us (even politicians) feel compelled to kiss and hug babies. The trick is to keep it up as your children grow older.

---

dren's health? You can't force yourself to love your wife, or your ex-wife, if those feelings are gone. What you can do, what you must do for the sake of your children, is to always treat her with respect and always speak of her with respect.

Your children don't need to hear you two squabble, and they certainly don't need to serve as sounding boards for any resentments or anger you still feel. Remember, your children's current and future well-being depends very much on how you deal with their mother.

Time

Good fathers not only give their children their love, they also give their time, and lots of it.

Beginning in the 1960s and on through the '70s and into the '80s, the unfortunate myth of "quality time" was perpetuated. Expert after expert appeared on talk shows telling parents not to worry if they had little time to spend with their children. How much time and attention children received from

their parents did not matter, as long as parents and children had "quality" interactions during the few minutes they spent together each day.

Quality time may have made millions of fast-track parents feel better about rarely seeing their children, but it also gave millions of children the message that they weren't worth much more than 5 or 10 minutes a day of their parents' time.

Telling children you regret you can't spend more time together doesn't make your children feel better; it just makes them think there's lots of other stuff in your life that's more important than they are. Making time for your kids says, "You're important to me" better than any words ever will.

The things you do with your kids don't need to be fancy. Simple events may be the most often remembered. So read a book together. Play a game. Visit a park and swing. Wrestle on the floor. Play catch. It really doesn't matter what you do together, as long as you spend time together doing something.

In today's busy world, finding the time to be with one's children can be difficult. One way you can make this time is to open up your schedule to your children's needs. Many men live by schedules. We like to get up at the same time, go to work at the same time, eat at the same time, and lie on the couch and watch TV at the same time. We just hate it when things get off schedule.

But your schedule should include much more than just meetings and business trips. It also should include taking your child to the pediatrician, reviewing homework each evening, and attending school events. You might even want to block off time every Saturday morning for just hanging out with your kids.

Another way to ensure you spend time with your kids is to find an organized activity, sign up, and do it together. The structure of Little League or piano lesson requires that child-father activities get written on the calendar that hangs on the kitchen wall.

Time Management: tips for busy dads

One of the most common complaints today is that there is never enough time, especially for the family. But not only is it possible to spend time with your children, doing so is absolutely critical to their healthy development. Here are some suggestions for managing your time so you can spend more of it with your kids:

☞ **Prioritize your time.** The biggest mistake people make is failing to prioritize their time. Example: At the office, rather than working on the big projects early in the day when they are freshest, many men work on their mail or phone call list. Later in the day, when they are tired, they try to turn to the important projects. The result: feeling overwhelmed by a "lack of time."

☞ **Keep a daily "To Do" list.** To help prioritize tasks, make a "To Do" list and prioritize the items on the list. Be sure to include both family and work activities for that day. Make sure your family comes out high on your list of daily priorities. Share this list with your family as a way to help keep you motivated to stick to your priorities and as a subtle means of emphasizing how high up they are on your list.

Don't worry if you don't finish all the things on your list; most people don't. The important thing is getting the highest priority items completed, and that should include spending time with your family.

☞ **Turn off the television.** Television is the great family-time killer. Limiting both your and your children's television viewing will greatly increase the amount of time you have available to spend with each other.

☞ **Eliminate time-wasting habits.** Many people spend too much time on activities that are relatively unimportant or could be accomplished in much less time. Example: Spending 45 minutes reading the newspaper, when a quick scan of the headlines will give you essentially the same information. It's a good idea to monitor your daily habits and search for ways to reduce the time you spend doing them.

☞ **Prepare for the day the night before.** Using the night before to prepare for the next day is a great time-saver, because it allows you to use the morning, when you are at your best, to accomplish the important tasks.

Examples: Lay out your work clothes for the next day before you go to bed. Put your coffeemaker on a timer so your wake-up brew is already made when you wake up. Organize your briefcase the night before and place it by the front door or in the car. Make your daily "To Do" list before you go to bed, instead of first thing in the morning.

☞ **Learn to do several things at once.** Many tasks take only a few moments, such as reading a memo or opening mail. Learn to use spare moments to get these tasks accomplished.

Examples: When put on hold during a telephone call, put the call on speaker phone and use the time to read a memo or open a letter. Take a small tape recorder with you when running errands or traveling in a car and create oral memos that can be typed up by you or your secretary later on.

☞ **Use e-mail instead of letters and phone calls.** The informality of e-mail means you will spend less time communicating compared to writing a letter or playing phone tag.

☞ **Delegate low-priority jobs.** Not everything needs to be done by you personally. The key to effective time management is delegating everything you can.

☞ **Fight the urge to be perfect.** Perfectionism is the enemy of time. Most tasks only require that they be "good enough," not perfect. Remember, your family is really job number one. When faced with a task that competes with family time, ask yourself: Which is more important, that this task be done perfectly or that I spend this time with my family?

And don't confuse neatness with efficient time management. Some people spend half their day organizing their desks. As long as your clutter is organized clutter, you'll do fine.

Or, sign up to be a chaperone for school field trips; your obligation to your child's school will ensure that you keep your date with your child.

It is also important to schedule family mealtimes. Eating well is important for your health, and eating together is important for the health of your family. If you and your wife work different shifts, it may be near impossible to schedule a family dinnertime, at least during the work week.

Too many families give up too easily, resulting in different family members eating dinner at different times of the evening, often in front of different television sets.

If you want to keep your family relationships strong, turn off the television, turn off the radio, put down the paper, and eat dinner together as many nights a week as humanly possible.

Even if you have to eat dinner at 8:30 at night because one of you gets home from work that late, do it. Your kids can survive on a nutritious snack until then.

Good things happen when families eat together regularly. Research by Diane E. Beals, Ed.D., at Washington University in St. Louis, found that children living in families who eat dinner together have more advanced language and reading skills compared to children whose families do not eat together regularly.

What does eating together have to do with language skills? Family mealtimes encourage conversation, which stimulates the development of children's verbal skills.

Bob Gilliam and son Shawn, 1974

Other research has found that children living in families who eat dinner together on a regular basis seem to have better family relationships and fewer emotional and behavioral problems than kids who tend to eat alone.

Don't think that you can wait until after your children are older to start having family meals. Even when your kids are babies you should be sitting down regularly to eat together. Habits become habits because you do them a lot. If, when your children are babies, you avoid having family meals, you will never develop the habit, much to your family's detriment.

We sit down to meals together on a regular basis—*even with 2-year-old twins. The thing about raising two 2-year-olds is that you can hardly control 'em. One 2-year-old, you can. But not two. You just do your best and make sure they don't get hurt. So our dinner table often looks like mealtime at the zoo—flying meatballs; a 2-year-old crawling across the table into his or her older brother's plate (2-year-olds are quick as rabbits!); little hot dogs flying across the table like SCUD missiles scoring direct hits on the vertical blinds, our oldest son, or my head. These are not so uncommon sights at our dinner table. There are times when my wife and I simply eat standing up as we jump to prevent one disaster after another. But we do it, most nights of the week, because it's important family time. (JR)*

We're not saying that every moment of your spare time needs to be spent playing with your kids.

As wonderful as being a father is, as great as kids are, we could think of no surer route to insanity and a failing marriage than to spend all of your time with your kids. But you should be available to your kids as much as possible.

When you are watching television, fixing the plumbing, or doing a little work on your home computer, allow your children to interrupt you.

If your children constantly hear, "Not now, I'm busy," they will eventually stop seeking you out. Then you will have lost out on the best part of fatherhood, which is having your children look to you for advice and help.

In fact, when you make yourself available to your children, you get several years of being admired by someone who actually thinks you know what you're talking about. Don't blow it by being too busy for your children. Magic often happens when you least expect it. If you want to experience it, you have to be there.

You just never know when something special will happen.

═══════════

I remember one hot August night, *driving home from a two-week vacation at the beach. We had brought so much stuff with us that we needed two cars to lug it all to and from the beach house we had rented. It was about 11:30 at night when we started off for our three-hour trek back home with my then 4-year-old daughter in the car my wife was driving and my 6-year-old daughter in the other car with me. I assumed my daughter would quickly zonk out in the back seat, and I was fumbling with some cassette tapes to listen to when my daughter asked, "When did you first know what you wanted to be when you grew up?" This simple question led to a nearly three-hour discussion of her dreams and fears about growing up, a conversation I will treasure for the rest of my life. (WH)*

═══════════

10 Ways to
make time for your children

1. Commit to a family mealtime each day.
2. Write your children's activities into your schedule book—in ink!
3. Identify one thing on your weekly schedule you can do without and replace it with kid time.
4. Take one of your children along when you run errands.
5. Volunteer to participate in a regularly scheduled child activity, such as coaching a softball team or helping with a school activity.
6. Identify one children's show on TV that you secretly like to watch and make a point of watching it with your child.
7. Develop an interest in a hobby you and your child can enjoy together.
8. If your work requires that you travel, take one of your children along with you when your business trip can be extended into a long weekend.
9. If your work schedule is flexible, start your work day earlier so you can get home earlier in the afternoon to be with your family.
10. Leave your work, cellular phones, and pagers at home when you go on family vacations and outings.

Commitments

Good fathers also understand the importance of keeping commitments. It's easy to break commitments. Any schmo off the streets can do that. The test of a good man is in his ability to keep commitments.

When you say you're going to be at your child's class play, be there. When you say you're going to take your child fishing this weekend, do it. Whenever you make a commitment to your children, make sure it is the last thing that gets canceled and not the first.

7 Reasons

why a good marriage is important to a child

1. It demonstrates how men and women should treat each other.
2. It teaches how to resolve conflicts successfully.
3. It helps teach what he or she should seek in future boyfriends, girlfriends, and marriage partners.
4. It teaches the value of commitment.
5. It demonstrates the importance of attending to the needs of others.
6. It provides a sense of security and stability.
7. Most of all: It demonstrates what it takes to sustain a healthy marriage.

Children are forever hearing "tomorrow … we'll do it tomorrow. I promise." Far too frequently, tomorrow never comes, and eventually your kids stop asking. Then it's too late. When it comes to your kids, don't put off until tomorrow what you know you should be doing today.

My oldest son gets more of my time than most kids get from their fathers, *not because I'm some sort of superdad, but because I work out of a home office. I take time from most workdays to pitch baseballs to him. I coach his baseball team. I go to school to cook gingerbread. But let me break one promise and his response is always the same: "You never keep your promises to me. You're the worst dad in the world."*

If I break one promise, no matter how good the reason seems to me, to him, I'm the Lex Luther of fathers. It doesn't matter what good things I did earlier in the day. Of course, when I let him eat an entire chocolate Easter bunny in one sitting, he tells me, with a straight face, "You're the best dad I've ever had."(JR)

Another suggestion is to commit to being there for the big events, such as birthday parties, class plays, baseball games, and musical concerts. Smaller events, such as watching your child's friend play baseball, deserve less attention from you.

It is inevitable that you will miss some of your children's big events. When this happens, ask your wife or someone else to videotape the event for you. Later, make the viewing of the videotape a special family event, rather than viewing it in private.

The other big commitment you have to keep is your commitment to your wife and your marriage. Marriage isn't easy. It takes work. But if you want your children to have the best start in life, commit to keeping your marriage strong and vital.

Don't be afraid—as many men are—to seek out periodic marriage enrichment programs. If there's a problem with your marriage, even if it's just a general sense of dissatisfaction, get some help. Seeing a marriage counselor or your rabbi, priest, or minister is not a sign of failure and weakness. It's a sign of commitment and strength.

A month before we got married, my wife and I (JR) went on a two-day Engaged Encounter retreat. It was held at a primitive church sanctuary during one of those oppressive Maryland heat waves. No air-conditioning, no television, no ESPN—to me, that's primitive. With the help of a married couple who volunteered to lead us and about 10 other couples through the weekend, we got to know each other more deeply than I had imagined possible.

I really liked what I discovered in my soon-to-be wife that weekend and, I guess, she kind of liked what she found in me. Thinking back to that weekend, it makes me realize that my wife and I are struggling now with one of the difficulties of parenthood: We're so exhausted by parenting three children and each running our own business that we don't get enough time to be a couple. But we know we're in this together for the long haul, so we keep plugging away.

> **Here's the best advice we can give about making and keeping commitments: Don't make too many. Really. Don't say you're going to play with your daughter later, if you know you probably won't. Don't say you'll read your son a bedtime story tomorrow, unless you know you will. Don't say you'll play catch with your kids in the backyard when you come home from work, unless you're reasonably sure you'll be home before dark. The best way to avoid disappointing your children is to make fewer promises, make only those you will keep, and keep all those you make.**

Responsibility

Good fathers take responsibility for the well-being of their children. This doesn't mean buying them everything in sight. It does mean seeing to it that they are well fed, well housed, and well clothed, and that they receive the necessary moral instruction to become persons of good character.

Accepting responsibility for ensuring the well-being of your children has no bearing on the question of who in the family works outside the home. Good dads come in many different forms. Some go to work each day. Others are stay-at-home dads, taking care of the kids while their wives go to work. Some couples work split shifts, an arrangement in which one works during the day and the other in the evening.

Decisions about who should work outside the home and when are decisions to be determined by each individual couple. Regardless of whether or not you work outside the home, being a good dad does mean measuring how any substantial decision you make about your own life will affect your children's well-being.

This may mean sacrificing a pay raise if your new job responsibilities would result in significantly less time with your kids. Or, it may mean deciding not to move to another area of the country for an attractive job offer because to do so would negatively affect your children's lives. Fatherhood is about sacrifice. Selfishness and fatherhood are mutually exclusive.

Wil Groves and son Jackson, 1988

A Word about Rocks

Being a father is the most important work you will ever do. You must be willing to step forward and say, "I will stand by and be supportive of my wife. I will make sure my children are well loved, fed, clothed, and safely housed. I will make sure they receive a good education and grow up to become persons of good character." It's a tremendous responsibility.

But fatherhood also has its rewards. Research has consistently shown that men who are involved family men are happier with their lives, are physically healthier, and are less likely to suffer from depres-

Find Time to commit to your children

If you're anything like the average man, your days are more than full. Where in the world are you going to find the time to be with your children? This handy chart should help.

Instead of...	Do this...
Watching TV	Play a game with your kids.
Talking on the phone	Talk with your children.
Finishing a report for your boss	Help your kids with their homework.
Staying late at the office	Go to work earlier so you can come home earlier to be with your children.
Watching sports on TV	Play sports with your kids.
Going to the ballgame with your buddies	Take your kids. Your buddies can take their kids, too.
Surfing the Internet	Take your kids swimming.
Reading the paper	Read your kids a bedtime story.
Working on a household project alone	Let your child do a similar project alongside you.
Gardening by yourself	Share gardening chores with your kids.
Doing office work at home	Do office work at home after the kids go to sleep.
Playing a weekly round of golf	Coach your child's youth league team.

cared for their children's intellectual and social development were actually more likely to advance in the workplace than men who did not.

Being a good father is also one way that any man can construct his own legacy. Most of us will never be rich or famous or write the great American novel, but each of us can help shape the future and leave a little something of ourselves behind by being a good father.

Then there are the more subtle, yet profound rewards. In the quiet moments, when you peek into the bedroom to watch your child sleep, there is a sense of satisfaction, knowing that you and your wife created that life and that you share responsibility for it. It's at those moments that you know, despite the spit-up on your clean shirt, the smell of the dirty diapers, and the bags under your eyes from lack of sleep, that being a dad is the best part of being a man. It's at those moments that you strengthen your resolve to do whatever it takes to be the best dad you can be.

Earl Weaver, longtime manager of the Baltimore Orioles and a member of the Major League Baseball Hall of Fame, once said: "Until you're the person that other people fall back on, until you're the one that's leaned on, not the person doing the leaning, you're not an adult. You reach an age when suddenly you realize you have to be that person. It could be elderly parents, children … anything. But one day you realize, 'It's me. I've got to be the rock.'"

Mostly, being a good dad is about being the rock.

sion compared to men who are disconnected from children and families.

A man's involvement with his children even contributes to occupational success. For example, in a four-decade study of 240 men born during the 1920s and 1930s, researcher John Snarey, Ed.D., professor of human development and ethics at Emory University in Atlanta, found that men who

being a good
prenatal
dad

Congratulations! You're a father. Once you and your wife found out you were expecting, you became a dad.

Really. Even if your wife hasn't yet given birth, you should start thinking of yourself as a dad. Get used to your important new status.

Your wife, obviously, is the pregnant one—and she feels like a mother already. Other than enjoying that great feeling of virility you get when your wife's ob-gyn says to her, "You're pregnant!," nothing much has changed for you yet. It's your wife who's going through all the changes. But let's face it. It's time for you to start acting like a dad.

David Gingold with sons Charlie and Benjamin, 1993

You might ask, what does a prenatal dad do? You're undoubtedly thinking that "prenatal dad" sounds like one of those silly pop psychology terms that get bandied about on afternoon talk shows and that we're going to suggest you wear a silly T-shirt that says something like, "We're pregnant!" or "I'm pregnant! My wife's just carrying the baby." Wrong! Sparing you from such nauseating advice is part of the reason we wrote this book.

The most important thing you can do as a good prenatal dad is to be understanding and supportive of your wife during the pregnancy. Remember that your wife will be living through powerful physical changes: weight gain, hormonal surges, her breasts getting ready for nursing. She'll also be going through emotional changes: ups and downs, anxiety about being a good mother, worries about the baby's health.

Pregnancy, while a wonderful experience, can be overwhelming, especially for a first-time mom. Your wife will need your understanding, patience, affection, and, of course, lots of help around the house. Research has shown consistently that the quality of the marital relationship is one of the strongest prenatal predictors of later childhood adjustment. In a study of more than 1,300 children and their families by researcher Dennis Stott, Ph.D., professor of psychology at the University of Guelph in Ontario, children conceived by and born to parents with a difficult marital relationship were almost 10 times more fearful and jumpy than the offspring of parents with happier marital relationships. At 4 or 5 years of age, these same children were also more likely to be undersize, timid, and emotionally overdependent upon their mothers.

Other studies have found that mothers with supportive husbands adjust better to their pregnancies, have more positive birth experiences, and give birth to less temperamentally difficult babies compared to mothers whose husbands are uninvolved in the pregnancy. So being a good prenatal dad means being a supportive husband. It's also your first step in being a good father.

It's important to keep in mind that for your wife, motherhood begins with conception. One of the biggest mistakes by a prenatal dad that we've ever heard of, was actually made by one of us:

When my wife was seven months pregnant, *I let Mother's Day come and go without so much as a word. As the day went by, I noticed my wife becoming more and more irritated. Finally, at the end of the day, she screamed at me, "It's Mother's Day. What do you think I've been doing for the last seven months, making chopped liver?!?!" (WH)*

So, important advice: If your wife is pregnant on Mother's Day, get her a gift.

Enjoy These Nine Months

If you are expecting your first child, you're in for a number of surprises, most of them good. Pregnancy is filled with many difficult moments for a woman, but contrary to television sitcom portrayals of pregnancy and your friends' horror stories, your wife will experience many wonderful moments as well. It's certainly not nine months of heaven. Pregnancy is hard work, but many women report that, for at least part of their pregnancy, they never felt healthier or happier.

The first month or even the first several months often brings morning sickness. No one knows what causes morning sickness, and there is no known cure. Some women report getting relief by drinking ginger ale or tea, eating saltine crackers, or sucking on lemons. If your wife experiences morning sickness, you can help by assisting her in experimenting with different kinds of foods to determine which ones produce the least amount of nausea. The rule of thumb is to help her get, as quickly as possible, whatever type of food that comes to her mind without accompanying waves of nausea. But don't force food on her; this will only make things worse.

Keep in mind that morning sickness rarely signals that something is wrong with the baby. Nonetheless, if the morning sickness is particularly severe, she may want to consult her obstetrician.

Usually, by no later than the 17th week of pregnancy, the morning sickness subsides. For a period of time after that your wife is likely to feel quite good. But in the last month or so, your wife's back will be killing her, and she'll be dying to "drop this baby." In fact, waiting for the baby to finally arrive can be the most frustrating and difficult time for both of you.

Of course, pregnancy also can be a completely wonderful experience for a woman, unaccompanied by either morning sickness in the early months or back pain in the final months. It can also be a wonderful time for you, too. "Yeah, how?" you might very well ask.

First of all, you and your wife can make love without worrying about contraception. There are two questions that pop into the head of all of us men upon hearing that our wives are pregnant: "Are my wife and baby healthy?" and, within a millisecond after getting a positive answer to that question, "Can we still have sex?" Yes, you can. Your wife should check with her ob-gyn, but barring any unusual circumstances, sex is fine during pregnancy for as long as it stays comfortable and enjoyable for you both.

You also get to enjoy the anticipation. If this is your first child, you will soon learn what nobody can really explain to you—the joy of being a father. We can tell you that being a dad is the greatest thing

in the world, a fantastic mix of fun, accomplishment, and hard work. But you won't even begin to understand what it's like until you have children yourself.

For now, you're going to have to take on some extra chores. As your wife's pregnancy proceeds, she won't be able to do much housework. Imagine, if

Tim Stilwill and daughter Carson, 1997

you would, trying to do a load of laundry or pushing a vacuum cleaner with a 15-pound bowling ball in your underwear. Not a pleasant thought, is it?

Plus, in the later stages of pregnancy women often begin to experience back pain. Chores such as lifting and pushing a vacuum become painful. So get to work. It's not fun, but it's important. And we can tell you, it is possible to master the manly art of high-speed cleaning. We have plenty of kids, we each have pretty big houses, and we can each clean the entire house in less than two hours!

The trick is to clean in stages and move fast. Don't work room by room; work chore by chore.

Dust the whole house—fast! Then vacuum the entire house—fast! Do the bathrooms next, moving from one bathroom to the next with all of your cleaning supplies in a container in one hand and a mop and bucket in the other. Finally, scrub down the kitchen. Voila! A pretty clean house in two hours or less. Besides, no one expects your house to be spotless during pregnancy.

Cleaning the house is necessary. Plus, many men feel left out during pregnancy. Taking on more work around the house will help you feel that you, too, are making an important contribution during your wife's pregnancy.

Develop Some Understanding

Pregnant women often experience wide mood swings. *Andy Griffith Show* reruns can make her burst out crying. If you don't eat three helpings of the dinner she cooked, she can start crying. A usually quiet woman can become as ferocious as a Pittsburgh Steelers linebacker when things don't go right. Or, an extremely competent woman can find herself sobbing uncontrollably, depressed at what she perceives to be her complete inability to do anything right.

Your wife is going through more than just emotional changes. The physical changes she is experiencing are pretty major. She'll be urinating frequently, especially during the first three months of pregnancy. And, as we mentioned, she may experience morning sickness—nausea, even vomiting—during the first several months.

Your wife will gain 25 to 30 pounds during pregnancy. This is healthy and most of the extra weight has nothing to do with increased body fat. It's due to increased blood and body fluids, and, of course, the baby. Indeed, your wife's doctor will be concerned if she doesn't gain enough weight. Your wife will be concerned about how she looks though. You can help her out by letting her know just how beautiful she is and how much you love her throughout this entire experience.

You may also want to take a look in the mirror yourself. Lots of men gain weight during their wife's pregnancy. Some even experience nausea, mood swings, and food cravings. The French have a word for it: *couvade*. It's also known as sympathetic pregnancy. If you gain weight, it could just be due to nervous eating—you know, "I'm nervous about having another mouth to feed, so I think I'll eat this quart of ice cream while watching TV!"

Bonding with Your Unborn Baby

Doctors used to believe that unborn babies were relatively passive and largely reflexive beings. However, we now understand that unborn babies develop much earlier than previously imagined and rapidly acquire a wide range of complex, sophisticated behaviors. For example, by the eighth week, your unborn child will be able to move his or her head, arms, and trunk. By the fourth month, your unborn child will be able to frown, squint, and grimace. By the sixth month, your unborn child will have acquired the ability to remember, hear, taste, and learn.

Your wife will naturally bond with your baby. As soon as your child is born, it will be obvious that Mom and Baby already know each other well. You, on the other hand, need to work at building a relationship with your baby while he or she is still growing in your wife's uterus.

Talk to your baby. That's right, lean over and talk to your unborn child right through your wife's belly. By the sixth month of pregnancy, your child's

Riding the emotional roller coaster

Our advice for dealing with your wife's emotional swings is to be very, very supportive. For more specific tips on dealing with emotions, consult this chart.

If your wife...	Do this...
Becomes upset that something's wrong in the house	Fix it. It may seem like nothing to you, but it's something to her.
Suddenly gets terribly worried about your unborn baby's health	Don't say, "I'm sure everything's OK." Instead say, "Let's give the doctor a call," or "Let's read up on what should be happening right now."
Breaks into tears over an *Andy Griffith Show* rerun	Give her a hug.
Expresses feelings of inadequacy	Listen carefully and help her remember how competent she really is.
Worries she'll be a failure as a mother	Give her a hug and remind her that if your mother (her mother-in-law) could raise a great son, then certainly she can do a great job.
Becomes angry at you for what seems to be no reason	Do your best to stay calm. On some occasions, it may help to go out for a walk.

your newborn, you'll be familiar and safe, which is important in the strange, bright, cold room into which he or she just got ejected.

When your baby emerges all wet and scrunchy at birth, don't let that be the first time your child meets you. Make sure you're not a stranger to your baby during these first nine months.

There are other important ways to build that father and child bond even before birth. Give your baby a good-night kiss. (Your wife will love it.) As your baby grows, place your hands on your wife's tummy and feel his or her movements. Sing to your baby. If you play an instrument, such as the piano or guitar, perform for your wife and unborn baby; there's a good chance your child will be born with a bit of appreciation for music.

Accompany your wife to her prenatal visits; if and when the doctor takes an ultrasound picture, you'll get to see your baby. Viewing the ultrasound is one sure way to enhance your attachment to your developing baby. One study, presented at an annual conference of the American Psychological Association, found that when fathers were able to view their unborn child via ultrasound, the level of the father's attachment to the unborn child increased.

ears have developed to the point where there's a good chance that they can hear.

Although the clearest sounds to the unborn child are those found in the uterine environment, the unborn child also can hear ambient sounds external to the womb, including voices. If you talk to your baby during pregnancy, after he or she is born, your baby will be able to recognize your voice. You won't be just another stranger in the delivery room. To

Interacting with your unborn child also can have enormous influence on your child's long-term development. This was demonstrated in one study of 54 middle-class couples done by Lewis E. Mehl, M.D., Ph.D., professor in the department of family practice and community medicine at the University of Vermont in Burlington. In this study, prenatal attitudes of the father toward his unborn child were among the most significant predictors of infant motor development at ages 2 and 6 months. Other studies show that fathers who interact with their children prenatally have children who later on show better emotional, intellectual, and motor development compared to children of fathers who do not. The road to Harvard starts in the womb!

Choosing a Pediatrician

Well before your baby is born, you and your wife should choose a pediatrician, a medical doctor who has received at least three years of specialized training in the treatment of children. Ask friends who have young children, colleagues, relatives, your doctor, and your wife's ob-gyn for recommendations. If you're insured through a managed-care plan, be sure to check the list of pediatricians who accept your plan's coverage.

Make an appointment to meet with each prospective pediatrician. Make sure you participate in these meetings. Choosing a pediatrician is not just a mother's job. It's one of the crucial ways you can help protect your child.

=====

In 1990, my then almost 2-year-old son was extremely sick. *Among other symptoms, he had a high fever that wouldn't go away. We had taken my son to see his pediatrician and consulted several times with the doctor over the phone. But by the sixth day, he was still sick. I brought him into the pediatrician's office again that morning. Dr. Shapiro examined my son and concluded that he had a rare, potentially serious illness. The disease is hard to diagnose, but if it's not treated within seven days of onset, it can cause permanent heart damage.*

Dr. Shapiro sent us right to the hospital. I remember arriving at the hospital and meeting almost immediately

Finding the
Right Doctor

When you interview a prospective pediatrician, here are several important questions to ask:

● What are the doctor's office hours?
● How many years has the doctor been in practice?
● Is the doctor (or the doctor's colleagues) available by phone 24 hours a day?
● If it is a group practice, how large is the practice, who are the doctor's colleagues, and how do they work together?
● What about referrals? Does the doctor have a good network of specialists to call on if necessary?
● Where does the doctor have hospital privileges? Is it at the hospital where your baby will be born?
● When will the doctor visit your baby at the hospital after birth?
● What insurance does the doctor accept?
You also should ask about any other special concerns, such as circumcising newborn boys, that you have.

with the pediatric cardiologist. As she explained what the disease could do to my son, I held him tightly and cried. It took several minutes before I could even speak. Treatment began right away and, thank God, it worked. My son beat the disease, and today he is just fine. I don't think a day goes by without my quietly thanking God that Dr. Shapiro and his since-retired colleague Dr. Paul diagnosed my son on the sixth day. (JR)

=====

Mostly, you will be deciding whether you are comfortable with the pediatrician. You'll be seeing the pediatrician you choose a lot over the next several years. In fact, if you're like most parents, by the time your child enters school, you will have seen or consulted your child's pediatrician more often than you will see or consult a physician for yourself during your entire adulthood. You need to feel that he or she is somebody you can talk to and who will listen to your concerns.

It is often a good idea to seek out a pediatrician who practices in a group. Then, if your pediatrician is on vacation or unavailable when your child gets sick, the group practice will have another pediatrician who is on call and available to take care of any medical emergency.

Some smaller towns or rural areas may not have a single pediatrician, let alone a group of pediatricians. In that case, you may have to seek another kind of physician, such as a family practitioner, for your child. That's not a problem. Just make sure the physician you choose has experience in the medical care of children.

If you're like most new dads, you will be fairly anxious about your baby's health. Some pediatricians will have telephone hours for such routine calls. Others may have nurses who screen these calls for them. Especially if this is your first baby, you want a doctor (or the doctor's nurse) who doesn't mind getting some anxious-dad phone calls.

Having a Healthy Baby

Your wife needs to follow a regular schedule of prenatal care. Her ob-gyn will want to see her once a month until her 28th week of pregnancy. After that, the checkups will be every three weeks for several visits, then every two weeks. Once your wife reaches the 36th week, the visits will be once a week until the baby is born.

You should go with your wife to as many prenatal visits as possible. Your wife will appreciate the support, and it's another way to bond with your baby. Certain visits are can't-miss ones for you: the first visit when your wife's pregnancy is confirmed and the visit when and if your wife's ob-gyn performs an ultrasound so you can see your baby.

Throughout the pregnancy, your wife's doctor will perform a number of tests. Blood and urine tests, for example, allow the doctor to keep tabs on the progress of the pregnancy and watch for any signs of potential problems with your baby's development. It's a good idea to go along with your wife to the doctor's office when the results of important tests are coming in. It can help alleviate her anxiety—and yours—and give you the chance to ask some questions.

There are a few other things you can do to help your baby enjoy a healthy nine months in the womb. The rule about no smoking and drinking during pregnancy applies to

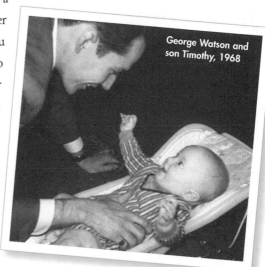

George Watson and son Timothy, 1968

you, too. "Huh?" you're thinking. Well, think about it. You and your wife started this baby thing together and quite enjoyable it was.

Now that your wife's pregnant, you need to keep working at it together. Your wife has to abstain from some things, and you should, too. It's a good way to support your wife and a good way to help your wife stay away from alcohol and tobacco. She'll know you're in her corner, working with her. And the research is clear: You don't want the mother of your child smoking or drinking when she's pregnant. It could be extremely dangerous to your baby.

You also need to protect your baby from secondhand smoke. The Environmental Protection Agency reports that breathing the smoke from other people's cigarettes, cigars, or pipes is almost as unhealthy as smoking yourself. Be forceful about keeping secondhand smoke away from your wife during pregnancy. Ask people to stop smoking and, if need be, leave any restaurant that can't seat you far away from smokers.

What You'll Learn in

a childbirth class

Why would you want to go to classes on childbirth? Isn't it enough that your wife goes? You might learn a few important things:

● What to expect in the later stages of pregnancy
● What your wife is really experiencing
● Ways your wife can feel more comfortable as pregnancy progresses and how you can help
● How your baby develops during pregnancy
● How to prepare your home for your baby
● Breathing exercises that will help your wife when the time comes to give birth
● How the doctors and nurses will monitor the health of your soon-to-be-born child during delivery
● What the various medications are for childbirth and what they're used for
● Common concerns and how to deal with them
● What to expect during your wife's hospital stay
● What you can do to help in the delivery room
● Tips on taking your baby home

Take a childbirth class together. You'll learn a lot about what your wife is going through and what the birth will be like. It's a good way to strengthen your partnership with your wife and your bond with your unborn child. The actual birth experience may be much different than what you'll learn in a childbirth class. (We'll talk more about this in the next chapter; there's no need to scare you too much at this point!) Suffice it to say, childbirth rarely proceeds in textbook fashion. We still highly recommend taking a class.

If your childbirth class doesn't take you on a tour of the maternity ward at the hospital where your wife will deliver, be sure to arrange a tour yourself. It's important that you familiarize yourself with the hospital so the surroundings do not intimidate you when your baby is being born. Besides, you'll need to know where the coffee and snack machines are, just in case the birth of your child is a long process.

You'll also want to get preadmission forms from the hospital. Most hospitals make it possible for you to fill out much of the paperwork at home and mail it in.

Be sure to familiarize yourself with your health insurance coverage. Find out how long a hospital stay your insurance will pay for. It used to be that many would only pay for a 24-hour stay following a normal delivery. But in September of 1996, the U.S. Congress passed a law requiring that insurance companies pay for a 48-hour minimum hospital stay after a normal delivery.

This extra day in the hospital gives the doctors and nurses 24 more hours to ensure that the mother and baby are doing just fine. And a new mom often appreciates an extra day of assistance from the nursing staff who can help her learn about feeding—especially breast-feeding—and baby care.

If you think your wife might need even more time in the hospital, you might want to find out what additional nights would cost you.

Getting the House Ready for Your Baby

If anything ever needed a "some assembly required" label, it's a baby! And the assembly starts before the baby's even born. From buying lots of diapers to picking out a crib and putting up wallpaper in the nursery, there's a LOT of work to be done.

This is a good time to practice the teamwork you and your wife will need to successfully raise children and

Pregnancy Tests: what they are and why they're important

Test	What it measures	What it's for	Intervention
Anemia	The amount of hemoglobin (oxygen-carrying protein) in the red blood cells	To find out if your wife has an iron deficiency	Doctor might prescribe iron supplements
Urine protein	Signs of preeclampsia or pregnancy-induced high blood pressure	These conditions can cause liver and kidney problems in the mother and premature delivery	Doctor might prescribe bed rest or early delivery
Diabetes	Blood-sugar levels	Diabetes can cause birth defects or an overly large baby that is difficult to deliver	Often is managed with a low-carbohydrate diet; sometimes requires insulin injections
Rh testing	The type of protein on the surface of your wife's red blood cells (most people are Rh positive)	If your wife is Rh negative, she may produce antibodies that can attack your baby's blood cells	An injection of Rh immune globulin (RhoGAM) is often administered during pregnancy
Toxoplasmosis	The presence of a parasite found in cat feces and raw meat	Can cause fetal brain, liver, or eye damage	If the test is negative (indicating that your wife has not developed immunity), she should avoid contact with cats and anywhere a cat is likely to roam (such as a litter box or in a garden) and avoid eating meat that is not cooked thoroughly
Sexually transmitted diseases	Syphilis, chlamydia, gonorrhea, hepatitis B	Can cause serious organ damage in infants and premature delivery	Treated with antibiotics; infants exposed to hepatitis B prenatally are immunized after delivery
Alpha fetoprotein	Levels of protein produced by your baby's liver	Large quantities may indicate a serious neural tube defect, such as spina bifida or anencephaly; low levels may indicate Down's syndrome	
Group B strep	Bacteria present in your wife's reproductive tract	In rare cases, can cause fetal death	Oral antibiotics may be prescribed
Amniocentesis	Extracts fetal cells from the amniotic fluid	To detect genetic defects such as Down's syndrome	
Ultrasound	A black-and-white image of the fetus created by sound waves passed through your wife's abdomen; often used as a follow-up to an earlier test	To calculate fetal age and check for multiple fetuses and structural defects	

A Word about cribs

A common job for dads is to put together the crib. Here are some safety tips:

☞ **Shop carefully.** To prevent infant strangulation or hanging, make sure the slats are spaced no farther apart than 2⅜ inches

☞ **Fit the mattress carefully.** The mattress should be firm and fit tightly in the crib so your baby will not get caught between the mattress and the crib.

☞ **Never use a pillow for a baby.** This can cause suffocation if your baby turns over onto his or her stomach and can't turn back over again.

☞ **Position the crib with safety in mind.** Never place the crib near anything that can be reached, such as drapery cords or venetian blinds.

Here's a list of some items you should stock up on before the Big Day arrives:

- 3–4 dozen newborn-size disposable diapers
- 3–4 diaper covers or plastic pants
- 1 diaper pail and plastic garbage pail liners
- a complete baby wardrobe, including pajamas, T-shirts, sweaters, socks or booties, and a sun hat
- 6–12 baby bottles and several day's supply of baby formula (even if your wife is breast-feeding, it is helpful to have some baby bottles around in case your wife does not produce enough breast milk or for when it's your turn to do the 3 a.m. feeding)
- a car seat (you'll need this for the trip home from the hospital)

---

maintain at least 65 percent of your sanity. In the months leading up to birth, your wife will spend a lot of time nesting.

What's nesting? When you come home from work or a trip to the store and find two dozen baby bottles neatly stacked on a kitchen counter, 15 baby-size washcloths folded just so in the linen closet, or new curtains in the family room, that's nesting. You'll know it when you see it.

You, on the other hand, won't be nesting, you'll be building. In most homes, the father builds the nursery and puts together the crib, changing table, and other pieces of furnishings. Just about anything that requires some assembly will be your job.

You and your wife also should spend some time stocking up on items you'll need after the baby is born. If this is your first baby, you may not realize just how much this new creature is going to dominate your life for the first few weeks. Between taking care of your wife and your baby, it is often difficult to find the time to go shopping.

So that's about it for being a prenatal dad. No silly T-shirts (well, that's up to you), just a lot of emotional support to provide your wife, some extra work around the house, and a great deal of excitement.

There will be some anxious moments, too, but that's normal. Sometimes you'll worry about the health of your unborn baby. If this is your first child, you'll worry about what kind of dad you will be. You'll wonder how well you and your wife will deal with all of the changes to come in your life. And, we can almost guarantee that you'll worry about the first time you hold your baby (What if I drop him or her?).

A bit of anxiety is to be expected. Deal with it by asking questions of your wife's ob-gyn and of friends and family who have been through this before and by talking to your wife.

These nine months will be hectic at times, but they will also be enjoyable and exciting. Our best advice is to be involved. Getting ready for your baby is almost as much your job as your wife's. If you're a good prenatal dad, you'll be well prepared for being a good father after your baby is born.

the birth

On the day your first child is born, your life changes forever. It will never be the same. You will never be the same.

You will be amazed at how much you can love one person—your child. As the years go by, you will be amazed at how great that love can grow. One day you think, "I couldn't imagine loving anyone or anything more than I love my child." The next day, you love your child even more.

Never before have you carried the responsibility you do now. It's a simple equation: Your value as a man rose astronomically once you had a child. The responsibility

Steven McDonald with son Nicholas, 1997

of raising your child to become a good man or woman rests on your shoulders (and, of course, on your wife's as well).

Think about it. When you played sports, the most valuable players on the team were given the most responsibility—the quarterback, pitcher, and shortstop, the center midfielder in soccer. It's the same in life. The most valuable men are those who can handle their responsibilities as a father and husband.

You probably have friends who became parents before you. They probably have said something to you like, "It's wonderful being a parent. But I can't put it into words. You can't know what it's like to be a parent until you are one." They're right. And you're about to find out just how right they are.

First, however, you and your wife are going to go through the most exhilarating, exhausting, frightening, and joyous day of your life. It's birth day.

Get Ready, Get Set

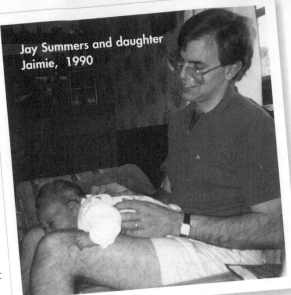

Jay Summers and daughter Jaimie, 1990

Although every pregnancy is different, the baby generally drops lower down into the pelvis several weeks before delivery. After this event, most women find they can breathe and eat more comfortably. That's the good news. Unfortunately, it also can mean greater lower back pain and more frequent trips to the bathroom as the baby exerts increased pressure on the bladder.

Soon after the baby settles lower, your wife will experience several physical changes that will let you and her know that labor is just a few days off:

● She will notice an increased, thickened vaginal discharge.

● The mucous plug that has sealed off the opening of the uterus (the cervix) is expelled.

● She may feel an intensification of what are known as Braxton-Hicks contractions. These are spasms in the lower abdomen that feel somewhat like labor contractions. Although they're uncomfortable, these contractions are usually shorter and weaker than the real thing, and they frequently stop with a change in position or activity.

Now's the time to make sure everything is ready. Is the hospital bag packed? Is the wallpapering done in the nursery? Do you have everything you will need when you bring home the baby? Do you have an infant car seat?

It's also time to let your employer know that your wife will go into labor any day now, and that you will soon be taking some time off. If you haven't already done so, make plans with your wife about how she can reach you any time of the day. If your job takes you out of the office and away from a phone, we strongly recommend renting a pager. We also suggest you tape your wife's ob-gyn's business card to each of the phones in your home, so you won't have to fumble through your phone book when you need to contact the doctor.

It's also a good time to have a romantic dinner with your wife celebrating the end of your couple-only relationship and the beginning of a newer, more exhausting, more fulfilling, more stressful, more joyous life together as parents. This romantic dinner will probably have to take place in the bed or on the floor with your wife lying on her side. And the fare will be determined by what your wife feels she can eat. Your romantic dinner could be buttered toast, grape juice, and a chocolate bar. You supply the romance with your attitude.

Soon you will be calling the doctor and, shortly after that, heading off to the hospital.

=====

Don't be too surprised if it takes more than a few days for labor to begin. *That's what happened to my wife and I when our first child was born. My wife's ob-gyn told us to expect labor within three days. Those three days happened to coincide with the dates the organization I worked for had their annual meeting out of town. I walked around the meeting telling everybody that I'd be leaving any moment. But, as each day went by and no labor, I became more and more tense.. On the third day of no labor, I was so tense I accidentally snapped the cold-water valve off the sink in the hotel bathroom. I didn't get to see the miracle of creation that day, but I did create quite a replica of Old Faithful and quite a plumbing mess for the hotel. My son was finally born a week later. (JR)*

=====

Your wife will know it's time to call the doctor when:
● Blood-tinged mucus discharges from her vagina.
● Her waters break. She'll know because of a gush or trickle of fluid that has nothing to do with urination.
● She feels contractions at regular intervals and the intervals gradually shorten.
● The intensity of the contractions gradually increases.
● She feels discomfort in her back and abdomen—more than usual.

This is not the time to put on your Indy 500 racing helmet just yet, but it's probably time to yell "Gentlemen, start your engines!"

Actually, you won't be rushing to the hospital. Your wife's doctor may ask her to come to his or her office at this point, rather than going directly to the hospital.

Usually, the doctor will want to see your wife once her contractions are five to six minutes apart and they have persisted for some period of time, say, an hour. The doctor will check how your wife and baby are doing and will determine how far labor has progressed. The doctor will also determine how much your wife's cervix has

dilated. (The cervix is fully dilated at 10 centimeters.) At this point, your wife's cervix is probably dilated just a few centimeters. This is the first stage of labor. It can last for several hours. Most of this first stage probably will be spent at home.

Resist the urge to rush to the hospital. If you're in doubt about when to go, your wife's doctor should be able to tell you. One of the most disappointing moments of a pregnancy can be arriving at the hospital and being sent home because your wife is not yet in active labor. If this happens, you'll need to help your wife deal with the disappointment.

=====

With our first child, we rushed to the hospital at the first sign of a contraction. *Of course, we were sent home, which was very disappointing to my wife, who was already a week overdue. To help get her mind off her now overdue pregnancy, we went to see the movie* Poltergeist, *and an hour later my wife began true labor. We're convinced that movie scared the baby right out of her. And I'll always wonder what possessed our ob-gyn to announce our daughter's arrival by saying, "She's heeree … ." (WH)*

=====

Based on the visit to the doctor and the frequency of the contractions, you and your wife will know when it's time to go to the hospital.

When Your Baby Is Overdue

Many parents place a great deal of significance on the mother's due date. When this date passes and there's still no baby, parents often become disappointed and worried.

It is important to remember that due dates are only estimates. They are not predictors of when your baby should be born.

In fact, half of all women do not go into labor until after their due date, and about 10 percent are still waiting for labor to begin two weeks afterward. A normal pregnancy can last anywhere from 38 to 42 weeks. Unfortunately, friends (and spouses) can make things worse for the mother by constantly asking, "Isn't that baby ever going to come out?!" or saying some other unhelpful nonsense.

Should your baby be "late," the most important thing is for you and your wife to stay in contact with her ob-gyn. If your wife's pregnancy does exceed 42 weeks, some problems can develop. At that point, the baby may suffer from malnourishment due to a deteriorating placenta, the nutrient delivery system that developed inside your wife's womb to feed the growing baby. Or, the baby may grow so large as to make delivery more difficult.

Consequently, it is a good idea for your wife to see that her doctor monitors the situation closely after the 41st week. It would not be unusual at that point for the doctor to want to see your wife twice a week. The doctor might want to do a test that involves strapping a fetal monitor onto your wife's abdomen. The doctor might order an ultrasound to check your baby's movement and muscle tone and the level of amniotic fluid inside the womb.

Your wife may also be asked to count the number of times the baby kicks in a 30-minute period (8 to 10 kicks every 30 minutes usually means everything is OK).

Some doctors routinely induce labor after about 42 weeks, although, if the cervix is thinning or beginning to dilate and the baby seems fine, many will continue to wait for labor to begin on its own. If there are signs of fetal distress, inducing labor or even an emergency cesarean section may be required.

So, if your wife is late, but your baby seems fine, just remind her (and yourself!) that good things come to those who wait.

Signals for early arrival

Signs that your wife may be going into labor too soon include:

● **Contractions.** Occasional contractions during pregnancy are normal. If they increase to more than five an hour, it may signal preterm labor. To determine whether your wife is having contractions, have her lie down and feel her abdomen below the navel. If it feels soft, it is not a contraction. If it feels firm to the touch, she is having a contraction. Call the doctor.

● **Backache.** Most women have backaches toward the end of pregnancy. Normal back pain will often subside when she changes position. With preterm labor, her back pain will not go away, even after she changes position. If the back pain is sudden or sustained, call the doctor.

● **Pelvic pressure.** Your wife may feel as if she needs to have a bowel movement but isn't able to. This may also feel like intestinal cramps.

● **Intestinal cramps.** These may feel like menstrual cramps and may be accompanied by diarrhea, nausea, or indigestion.

● **Change in vaginal discharge.** Report to your doctor any change in consistency, color, or amount of vaginal discharge, especially if the discharge is pink or red.

Born Too Soon

The flipside to a baby being overdue is a baby who comes too early. About 8 to 10 percent of all infants are born too soon. Risk factors for a premature birth include a history of preterm births; twins, triplets, or other multiple births; infection; uterine abnormalities; too much amniotic fluid; lack of regular prenatal care; and poor diet during pregnancy.

You can help your wife avoid going into labor too soon by making sure she:

- doesn't lift or carry anything weighing more than 24 pounds
- gets plenty of rest
- keeps stress to a minimum
- maintains a healthy diet and gains enough weight during pregnancy
- avoids alcohol, tobacco, and caffeine
- schedules visits with her ob-gyn regularly throughout the pregnancy

If your wife does go into preterm labor, she may still be able to avoid giving birth prematurely by curtailing her activities and entering a period of complete bed rest. Sometimes doctors will prescribe a labor-inhibiting drug or in extreme cases will stitch the cervix closed.

Premature births should be avoided because if the baby is born too soon some of the internal organs, especially the lungs, may not be ready to work right after birth. The good news is that due to advances in medicines, many premature infants do well and show no signs of long-term problems. In fact, even when babies are born after only 30 weeks, more than 90 percent survive and only 1 in 5 babies has any long-term problems. By the 35th week, the survival rate increases to 99 percent, and only about 3 percent experience long-term difficulties.

Welcome to the Hospital

It's not like in the old days, when the father waited outside on the porch, pacing back and forth, or sat on the stoop, nervously chewing on a corncob pipe, while, inside, the women boiled water and delivered the baby. Nowadays, modern medicine has important work for you to do the minute you and your wife enter the hospital—paperwork.

That's right. It may be the miracle of creation, but you don't get to participate in that miracle until the paperwork's all filled out. If you filled out much of the paperwork and delivered it to the hospital earlier in your wife's pregnancy, you're ahead of the game, but you'll still have a bit of paperwork to deal with.

Depending on how your wife's feeling, she can sit and wait while you do this. Or, you may be able to take her up to the labor and delivery room, get her settled, then return to the admitting office to complete the forms.

Do whatever you can to make the time spent with the person from the admitting office as low-stress and as quick as possible. You will be nervous, and you will be anxious to get up to where the action is. The last thing you want to do is fill out forms. Here are some suggestions to help this stage go smoothly:

☛ **Do your homework.** Check out the requirements of your insurance company in advance. What labor and delivery benefits do they cover? Do they require preauthorization for nonemergency hospital stays for labor and delivery?

☛ **Bring the necessary documents.** Know what you will need and make sure, in advance, that it's handy. This may include insurance cards and Social Security numbers.

☛ **Do your accounting ahead of time.** Know in advance what you're buying that your insurance won't pay for. If you're paying for a private postpartum room or for an extended stay, know what it will cost. Know how you will pay for it. If you're paying by credit card, have the credit card handy.

Once your wife is admitted, she and your soon-to-be-born baby will be evaluated by a nurse. Your wife's vital signs will be checked. This includes blood pressure, temperature, pulse, and respiration. The nurse will record the frequency and strength of the contractions and will note how far your wife's cervix has dilated. The nurse will also determine the baby's position inside your wife's pelvis and whether the baby's heart is beating at a normal rate and rhythm.

Your job at this point is to help make the labor or birthing room as comfortable for your wife as possible. If your wife brought along a picture or some other object for a focal point (something she can concentrate on during the toughest stages of labor), put that up. Unpack the items from your wife's bag that she'll be needing during labor and delivery, such as her robe and any reading materials she might have brought along. When you get a moment, check out where you will be able to get cold water and ice chips for your wife. When she yells for ice chips, you want to know exactly where to go and the quickest way to get there.

What Is Labor Really Like?

Not too many years ago, scientists in Montreal asked a variety of people to rate their individual type of pain on a scale of 0 to 40. Arthritis pain scored about a 15, cancer pain was rated 25, and labor pain for a first-time mother hit 35.

Although pain cannot be avoided during childbirth, there are ways to manage it, even before you get to the hospital. Your active involvement in your wife's labor preparation can help reduce her anxieties about childbirth. This is important because when a woman enters labor tense and fearful, it can cause a reduction of blood flow and oxygen to the uterus, inhibiting dilation of the cervix and making labor more difficult and painful.

Your job is to come to childbirth prepared with a good knowledge of the options available for helping manage your wife's pain. It is a good idea to talk over these options with your wife well ahead of time. But you both should realize that it is impor-

What Is fetal monitoring?

Your wife's doctor will want to monitor how well your baby is doing while your wife is in labor. Fetal monitoring, using either an external or internal device, measures your baby's heart rate, letting the doctor (and you) know if your baby is experiencing any unusual stress.

There are two types of fetal monitoring. The most commonly used is known as external fetal monitoring. This involves wrapping a belt with a monitoring device around your wife's abdomen. Internal monitoring involves inserting a long, narrow device through your wife's cervix and attaching the monitor directly to the unborn baby's scalp. Internal monitoring is used when the external monitor is not providing a good report or in high-risk pregnancies.

Even the internal monitor is harmless to your child. It doesn't seem to hurt, though after your baby is born, you may see a small mark on his or her scalp. This mark quickly heals and disappears.

tant to stay flexible when the Big Day actually arrives.

There's no way to predict what labor and delivery will be like for your wife. The childbirth experience varies not only from woman to woman, but also from pregnancy to pregnancy.

My wife's experiences were on the easier end of the spectrum. *Both times, labor lasted 10 to 12 hours and, while it was painful and extremely hard work, the labor and delivery progressed as smoothly as can be expected. (JR)*

My wife's first delivery did not go smoothly. *Labor lasted 36 hours, including three hours of hard pushing. It was horrible for her. It was horrible for me, watching her suffer so much and* *being able to do so little to help. We were expecting the worst when my wife went to the hospital two years later to deliver our second child. Determined to avoid a repetition of the first delivery, my wife requested and was given pain medication orally shortly after arriving at the hospital. Our second daughter arrived 30 minutes later after only two pushes—a birth so quick that the pain medication had not yet had time to take effect. (WH)*

An encouraging note: For your wife, all the pain of labor will cease immediately after the moment of birth. It's getting to that moment that's the challenge.

Your Role During Delivery

Delivering a baby can be an extremely difficult experience for your wife. Regardless of how nervous you are and how worried you are about your wife's health and your baby's health, you have got to be a rock for your wife. No matter what.

You two created this baby together. Now you're going to deliver this baby together. You are not in the birthing room to be an observer. You are there to assist and be an advocate for your wife. If she needs something, make sure she gets it. If there's a problem, make sure it gets fixed. Ask questions of the staff. If need be, give

Helping with pain relief

There are many ways to manage pain during childbirth. Here's a rundown of several ways you can help:

Method	How
Help your wife take a bath or shower	Warm water can be relaxing. Early in labor your wife may find it helpful to sit in a warm bath or take a warm shower. Some hospitals have even installed labor pools in their birthing rooms. But don't let her soak after her amniotic membrane has broken; doing so can risk infection. At that point, warm washcloths placed on her forehead can help.
Play music for your wife	It is said that music soothes the soul. Listening to music during labor can help your wife relax. Bring a portable cassette or compact-disk player with your wife's favorite music.
Create a relaxed environment	Keeping the lights low and the room as quiet as possible can be helpful to some women. Others prefer distractions.
Give your wife a massage	One of the most important tools you have in helping your wife through labor is your hands. Reach out and touch her, wherever and whenever she needs it.
Help your wife with her breathing exercises	There are many different breathing techniques that can be helpful, including the old standby "pant-pant-pant, blow-blow-blow." Your childbirth class will teach them all. Practice several methods, since you will never know which one will help the most.
Time the contractions	Your wife may find it helpful for you to time her contractions and talk her through them, almost like a sportscaster ("Here it comes … OK, it's peaking now … there the pain is going, going, gone! Good.")

Pain Relief from the doctor

The most effective weapons in the pain relief arsenal belong to the doctor. Here's a rundown of what he or she can do to help during childbirth:

Type	What it does	Considerations
Anesthetic	Blocks sensation and movement	Only reduces the pain; does not eliminate tension and muscle tightness. Effects can vary; provides significant relief for some women, little relief for others. If used before active labor begins, it can stall the labor's progress.
Narcotic	Reduces pain without reducing movement. Some commonly used narcotics include Sublimaze, Demerol, Nubain, and Stadol.	Can pose some risks to the baby, including changes in heart-rate patterns. Stays in the baby's system longer than in the mother's system, causing sluggishness after birth.
Epidural	A regional anesthetic injected near the spinal cord. Numbs the body from the midsection down while allowing the mother to remain fully aware of what's going on around her. Usually contains both an anesthetic and a narcotic.	May suppress the urge to push, thus prolonging labor and increasing the risk of a cesarean section. Can cause backaches for as long as several months after birth of the baby. Does allow the woman to be awake, even during a cesarean. Provides effective pain relief within 5 to 15 minutes. Generally regarded as safe for the baby. Is expensive, costing between $500 and $1,500. Not all hospitals can guarantee that an epidural will be available at the time of labor, since it requires an anesthesiologist to be present.

directions to the staff. It's your job to make this experience as comfortable (tolerable may be a better word) as possible for your wife.

That means that you have a role to play in the delivery room. A good ob-gyn will treat you as a partner in the birth. Act like a partner. For example, your wife will need to make a decision about pain medication. It will be helpful to both the ob-gyn and to your wife if you participate in that decision.

If she's in severe pain and labor is difficult and progressing slowly, urge her to take some pain medication. There's no right or wrong decision here. Delivering with or without pain medication is a

choice to be made by you and your wife; neither option is better than the other. And medications used today for pain relief usually have no long-term negative effects upon the baby. (It's a good idea to be well-informed about pain medications before you go into the delivery room. This is not the best time to be asking for the pros and cons of each, but by all means ask any questions you need to ask.)

It's also a good idea to keep in mind that no matter what kind of decision you and your wife have made ahead of time, you need to stay flexible. It's her body and her pain, and you can't possibly know what it feels like. If you've agreed on a "natural birth" ahead of time, be aware that she may change her mind and decide she wants pain relief.

By the time you and your wife arrive at the hospital, she will be approaching the end of her first stage of labor. The first stage ends with a transitional phase, during which the cervix dilates 7 to 10 centimeters.

Ten centimeters is the magic number. That's when your wife officially enters the second stage of labor. It's time to push this baby out! And it's time to help and encourage your wife as she gets the job done. She'll need help maintaining the best position for pushing.

Encouraging your wife to push should be your job, along with a nurse, if necessary. Most likely, the nurse will be helping support your wife from one side and you from the other. You and the nurse will each be holding one of your wife's legs, and each of you will be offering words of encouragement as your wife pushes.

A couple of words on what you learned in childbirth class: Childbirth classes are a good idea. But here's the secret about childbirth classes that nobody tells the fathers: The class will give you lots of specific instructions about coaching your wife during delivery. But when labor finally hits, your wife will tell you exactly what to do, and often it will have little if anything to do with what you paid to learn in a childbirth class. Ideas and techniques that sounded great in class may be worthless during the real event. The key is to be flexible and improvise.

What's a man to do?

If you've never felt helpless before, sitting next to your wife while she's in labor should introduce you to that feeling. You can't take away the pain. You can't make the process go any faster. So what can you do? Here are a few suggestions:

Do this in the birthing room ...	Don't do this ...
Be an active participant. Make sure your wife knows you're there with her, helping and supporting her the best you can.	Put a football game on TV in the birthing room, unless, of course, your wife enjoys watching football, in which case it can help distract her.
Advocate for your wife. If something's bothering her, get it fixed.	Suggest your wife push the nurse call button.
Listen to your wife. Pay attention to her needs.	Say, "That's not the way we practiced it in childbirth class."
Help your wife make a decision about pain medication; be an active participant in this decision.	Stand by quietly and passively.
Take part in the action: Support your wife. Run to get ice chips. Help her through contractions and pushing.	Faint.
Hold your newborn baby.	Stay fainted.
Cut the umbilical cord (with the doctor's permission).	Say, "Oooh, gross."
If you want to take a photo or shoot a bit of video, do so after the baby is born.	Spend all of your time taking pictures of your wife during labor and delivery.

My wife told me to *"shut up with your stupid breathing techniques ... don't say a (expletive deleted) word. Just fan me!" (JR)*

Episiotomy: painful, but often important

One of the most uncomfortable sights you may see during delivery is something called an episiotomy, a procedure that involves cutting the area between the vagina and the anus (the perineum) with surgical scissors. Doctors do this in order to enlarge the vagina to prevent tearing of the perineum and speed delivery.

Although more than half of all first-time moms will be given this surgical procedure, some doctors now question whether it is routinely necessary or even desirable.

Research published by the American Association for the Advancement of Science suggests that women who receive an episiotomy are 21 times more likely to experience severe perineal tearing during subsequent births compared to those who do not. Furthermore, women who do not have an episiotomy tend to heal faster, resume sexual intercourse earlier, and have less pain during intercourse than those who do have an episiotomy.

Should you and your wife decide you want to avoid an episiotomy, here are things you should do:

☛ **Talk to the ob-gyn beforehand.** Your wife needs to let her ob-gyn know she prefers to avoid an episiotomy if possible. She should let her ob-gyn know you both have read research that suggests a perineum tear will heal faster than a perineum cut.

☛ **Learn what you can.** Take instruction from a childbirth class that emphasizes what's known as soft pushing and gives instruction in perineum massage. Hard-pushing techniques are more likely to cause significant tearing, and perineum massage can help soften the tissue prior to childbirth.

Some doctors suggest that not having an epidural will help increase a woman's control over pushing during childbirth. This can help your wife coordinate her pushing with the instructions of the ob-gyn.

There are times when an episiotomy is required. When a baby is showing signs of fetal distress, a quicker delivery may be required. Even if you plan not to have an episiotomy, do not take it as a sign of failure or lack of cooperation on your ob-gyn's part if your wife has to have one.

Throughout her pregnancy, *my wife and I dutifully practiced the breathing and focusing techniques we had learned in our childbirth classes. Thus, we arrived at the hospital prepared for anything—anything, that is, except for 18 hours of hard labor, including three full hours of pushing. Toward the end of the second hour of pushing, my wife turned to me and said softly, "Get a gun and shoot me." Touched by her heroic attempt at humor at such a difficult time, I laughed. She responded by grabbing the collar of my shirt, pulling me within half an inch of her face and, screaming, "I said, 'Get a gun and shoot me!'" (WH)*

Final, Glorious Moments

Eventually, your baby's head can be seen during and after a contraction. This is called crowning. It's an exciting moment when the doctor proclaims, "I see the head." By all means, lean over and take a look when you hear this. It's a pretty amazing sight.

Soon your baby's entire head will slide out, usually with the face down. Then the baby turns and emerges one shoulder at a time. The doctor then pulls the baby out, and there you go: You've got a baby!

Make sure you take this opportunity to continue bonding with your child. Believe it or not—and most men don't believe it before the fact—when you first see your child emerge from the birth canal, you will forget about all the blood and other body fluids and see only the face of your newborn child.

There are a few peak experiences in life: hitting your first home run, getting your first car, your first date. This is one of them. Savor the moment. Then quickly give your wife a kiss. She's just been through hell—a glorious hell, indeed, delivering a child, but hell, nonetheless. She deserves and has earned your love and affection.

Greeting Your Baby

The moment when you first meet your baby can barely be described. It really is one of life's rare, exhilarating moments.

A visitor from another planet might look at your newborn, shudder, and think, "Ugh, what a slimy, scrunchy little thing these humans begin as." But to us humans, a newborn, covered as he or she is in slippery white stuff (called vernix) and with a slightly misshapen head from squeezing through the birth canal, is one of the most precious sights in this world.

Yes, a new baby is one of the most precious sights in this world. But in all honesty, first-time parents can be a bit taken aback by the first look at their newborn. We all envision a fresh-faced Gerber baby when imagining our soon-to-be-born child. But newborns don't look like the baby pictures on the front of baby food jars. For some fathers, the squishy, head-slightly-misshapen baby looking up at them can cause some discomfort. (Why don't I think my baby is the cutest thing in the world?) If you have this experience, don't worry. It's perfectly natural and, as your baby develops, he or she will become the cutest thing in the world.

One of the first things the ob-gyn will need to do after the baby emerges through the birth canal is

Cesarean Section
what if your wife needs one?

Far too many deliveries these days are done by C-section: almost 25 percent of all births. Medical experts estimate that somewhere around 1 in 6 is probably a more reasonable rate.

There are good reasons to deliver by C-section. A baby who is too large for the mother's pelvis presents a good example. And emergency C-sections are sometimes necessary, if, for example, the umbilical cord becomes compressed or entangled so the baby's blood and oxygen flow becomes constricted. Here are some tips for making sure that, if delivery takes place by C-section, it's for an appropriate reason:

Sometime during the third trimester—but before the 36th week—you and your wife should discuss C-sections with her ob-gyn. Find out about the criteria the doctor uses when deciding whether to recommend a C-section versus vaginal delivery. Discuss when a C-section should be considered and how the decision would be made. Above and beyond these criteria that you've discussed ahead of time, your doctor also should agree to call for a C-section only in an emergency situation.

Also find out whether you will be allowed to be in the operating room with your wife should she deliver by C-section. Many hospitals will allow this for a routine C-section. Discuss this with your wife as well. Ask her how she will feel about you being in the operating room. Remember, if you're not there, you won't see your child being born.

cut the umbilical cord. Your wife's doctor may allow you to do the cutting then present your child to your wife. Check this out with the ob-gyn beforehand. If the doctor says it's OK, then do it. That way, you get to complete the act of bringing your baby fully into the world.

Don't be surprised if soon after the birth, the doctor or a nurse suctions the mouth or nose of

Newborn tests and measurements

In addition to the one-minute and five-minute Apgar screening, hospitals commonly perform the following tests on newborns:

Test	Why it is necessary
Height, weight, and head	Physicians have charts indicating what circumference is normal and what isn't for a child's gestational age (the age since conception not birth). These are gross measures of development. If, for example, a baby's head circumference is either much too big or much too small, it could indicate a problem with his or her brain development.
Eye prophylaxis	Physicians routinely administer a small amount of antibiotics into the eyes of newborns to protect against serious eye infection caused by exposure to gonorrhea in the birth canal. This is done routinely because mothers can carry the gonorrhea virus without showing any symptoms.
Vitamin K injection	Usually within the first few hours of birth, your baby will be injected with vitamin K, a vitamin necessary for blood clotting. Babies lack this vitamin until after they have been fed for a few days and acquire a bacteria in their intestines that is necessary for synthesizing vitamin K. The shot protects the baby against hemorrhagic disease, a rare but potentially serious bleeding disorder.
Blood tests	All states require screening for phenylketonuria (PKU), a rare disorder that can cause mental retardation if not detected early. To test for the presence of PKU, a small amount of blood is drawn from the heel of the newborn soon after his or her first feeding. If the test is positive, the child will be placed on a special diet that will allow the child to develop normally. Some hospitals also routinely test for hypothyroidism (a rare disorder in which the body produces insufficient thyroid hormone) and galactosemia (another rare disorder in which the child is unable to digest carbohydrates in milk).
Hepatitis B vaccine	Newborns are given this shot before discharge from the hospital to guard against hepatitis B infection.
Hearing exam	Increasingly, newborns are being tested for inner ear problems prior to release from the hospital. The test consists of inserting a small probe into the newborn's ear canal.
Physical exam	Within the first 24 hours, then again before discharge from the hospital, the physician will perform a complete physical exam of your baby. The doctor will check your baby's breathing, listen to his or her heartbeat, feel the baby's pulse, examine his or her skin color (blue skin can mean circulation problems, and yellowish eyeballs and skin tone can indicate jaundice, a common condition caused by a chemical imbalance in the blood), and check for the presence of certain baby reflexes. The doctor also will check to be sure your baby has passed urine within the first 24 hours and a stool within 48 hours.

your baby. They do this to ensure a clear passageway for your baby to breathe. A nurse will then swaddle your baby in a blanket to keep him or her warm. No matter how hot and sweaty you may feel from all of the excitement, to your newborn child the hospital's a pretty cold place compared to Mommy's womb. Plus, it can take a while for a newborn's body temperature to stabilize.

If you brought a camera into the birthing room, now is the time to take it out (not before—remember, you are a participant in this birth, not a professional photographer). Snap a picture of Mommy and your new baby. Better yet, have one of the nurses take a picture of all three of you.

Now your wife will complete the third stage of labor, the afterbirth. That's when she expels the placenta. Most men are too preoccupied with their newborn at this point to notice.

The first visit with your new baby will seem too short. The doctor and nurses will need to clean your baby up, weigh and measure him or her, and do some tests to make sure everything is OK.

One test they frequently perform right in the delivery room is called the Apgar score. This test is a simple screening measure, named after Virginia Apgar, M.D., a Columbia University professor and physician who developed it more than 40 years ago.

The Apgar score is administered twice, once at one minute and once at five minutes after birth. It provides a measure of how your baby is responding to his or her new surroundings. Basically, it assesses your baby's heart rate, muscle tone, breathing, reflex response, and skin color, each on a 0 to 2 scale. Healthy babies get a score between 8 and 10, especially at the five-minute mark.

If your baby gets a lower score, don't worry too much. Apgar scores are used primarily to determine whether or not your baby needs any immediate medical intervention and do not predict how intelligent or healthy your child will be later in life.

The Circumcision
decision

Should you have your son circumcised? That is a personal decision you and your wife will have to make. Although there are many good reasons to choose circumcision, there is no right or wrong answer to this question.

More than half of all boys born today in the United States are circumcised. Fathers often want their sons circumcised because "I'm circumcised and so are my brothers" or because they don't want their sons to look and feel "different" from the other boys in the locker room. Other parents decide on circumcision for religious reasons. In the Jewish faith, for example, a religious ceremony called a bris is held when the boy is 8 days old, and the circumcision is performed by a special member of the faith called a mohel.

The American Academy of Pediatrics reports there are medical reasons for having your son circumcised, including: Circumcision lowers a child's chances of developing a urinary tract infection before age 1 year; men who are circumcised have a lower chance of contracting a sexually transmitted disease or of contracting penile cancer; and genital hygiene is easier to maintain.

The American Academy of Pediatrics also points out, however, that almost all boys who were not circumcised can be taught proper hygiene, especially how to wash underneath the foreskin, so as to lower their chance of getting infections.

The decision is basically up to you and your wife. If you haven't made the circumcision decision before birth, make it within a day or two. Unless religious laws dictate otherwise, circumcision is usually performed within the first few days of life.

Circumcision is a safe procedure. Complications are rare. If you and your wife have any questions, talk to your baby's pediatrician.

You and your wife and—if everything checks out all right—your baby will spend the next couple of hours in the recovery room. During this time, your wife's vital signs will be monitored to make sure

Taking Your
new baby home

Here are some things to remember before you bundle your newborn up for the drive home:

☛ **Check that car seat.** Make sure you have an infant car seat and make sure it is properly installed in your car. Read the instructions. Too many children get hurt because the car seat was not properly installed.

☛ **See to your wife's wardrobe.** Make sure your wife has a fresh, clean, attractive outfit to wear home. You may need to bring something from home.

☛ **Collect those "freebies."** Bring home everything the hospital gives you. All this stuff was part of the service you paid for. This can include extra diapers, pacifiers, glucose water, etc.

☛ **Clean up after yourself.** Make sure your wife and baby are coming home to a clean house. The moment you and your wife carry your child into the home is a grand moment, but it will lose some of its luster for your wife if she comes home to an empty pizza box in front of the TV and a pile of dishes in the sink. (Besides, you've just brought home from the hospital a brand-new, professional messmaker.)

☛ **Be romantic.** Arrange to have flowers or some other special gift waiting at home for your wife.

☛ **Don't plan a surprise party.** It is highly unlikely your wife will want visitors. Plus, this is a special time for you, your wife, your baby, and your baby's siblings, if any. Keep the celebration to the immediate family.

There will be plenty of time to visit with your newborn child during the next one or two days at the hospital. The hospital should allow unlimited visiting hours for dads. Some hospitals will even allow fathers to spend the night.

I have to be honest. *I had no desire to spend the night. I knew I was looking at the last night of quiet in my house for years and years to come. I went home and enjoyed it: late-night pizza, baseball on the television. But don't tell my wife. I think I said something about going home to make sure the house was in order for their arrival the next day. (JR)*

An increasingly popular option is having the baby stay in the same room with the mother. Not only does this allow the baby more interaction with his or her brand-new parents, but it also allows first-time moms and dads to learn how to take care of their newborn by observing the nurse doing so. Still, some moms prefer to rest after delivery, especially if they have had a cesarean delivery, and have the baby spend at least some of the time in the hospital nursery.

Don't be afraid to use this time to ask the nursing staff questions about your baby, such as how to take care of the umbilical cord, how to change the diapers, even tips about breast-feeding. Unfortunately, babies don't come with built-in instruction manuals. That's why God invented nurses!

Before you have a chance to get used to your baby, it's time to take him or her home. We happen to know, based on knowledgeable sources, that the Food and Drug Administration is considering requiring a label on every newborn: "Caution: In laboratory tests, newborns have been shown to cause excessive coffee consumption in adults." Which leads us to the next chapter, "The First Two Weeks," perhaps better titled, "The U.S. Armed Services Sleep-Deprivation Training Manual."

everything is OK. If she has had an epidural, she will be monitored closely in the recovery room until the effects of the medication wear off and feeling returns to her legs.

Meanwhile, you can spend the time cooing over the most beautiful baby ever to grace this planet.

the first two weeks

Warning!

Your new baby is going

to make a lot of noise!

We know, we know. You pictured this beautiful baby—the most beautiful baby that ever graced this planet—coming home with you and sleeping like, well, like a baby.

Sure, you figured you might have to rock your baby gently to sleep once in a while. But the really hard work—getting that baby through your wife's birth canal—is over with. Now you can relax, right?

Brad Hong with daughter Aimee, 1985

Baby bowel movements

Something that worries a lot of parents of newborns is whether or not their baby is having normal bowel movements. Here's the lowdown.

Almost all healthy newborns within 24 hours of birth have what's known as a meconium stool—a greenish black, tarlike bowel movement that clears out all the stuff their intestines have been accumulating during pregnancy.

After that first bowel movement, newborn babies will begin to have other, equally unusual-looking stuff appearing in their diaper. But this next phase of baby dooty may not begin for several more days, despite feeding on lots and lots of milk or formula.

Some parents worry so much about this lack of bowel movement they are tempted to give their baby a suppository. Don't.

Perfectly healthy babies may not have a second bowel movement until five or six days after the meconium stool. If you are worried, call your pediatrician. Remember: The only dumb question you can ask a pediatrician is the one that never gets asked.

Not exactly. When your baby is awake, most of the time he or she will be crying. This is not a soft, plaintive cry, but an urgent, red-faced, trembling, "I think I'm going to stop breathing" cry.

Some babies get so agitated and worked up that they even throw up.

Don't worry, there's nothing wrong with your baby. He or she has just been abruptly evicted from the ultimate baby resort, the womb, and dumped into some bright, noisy, cold, and strange world. You'd cry, too.

So if you're a first-time dad, this will be your first experience with long-term sleep deprivation—unless, of course, you've been through military survival training.

The reason babies cry so much is that all that bluster is the only way they can communicate their needs to you. Babies have at least three different cries: the hunger cry, the pain cry, and the anger cry.

After spending a few months with your baby, you'll be able to tell what your child is trying to communicate with each of his or her different cries. Well, most of the time, that is. Sometimes, unfortunately, it will simply be impossible to tell why your baby is crying.

Your newborn is, after all, just a baby, and there will be times when he or she will cry just for the sake of crying. Or because you forgot to turn on the baby mobile in the crib.

Here are two good rules about crying to keep in mind:

Crying Rule Number One: You can't spoil a baby. You can spoil an older child, but you can't spoil a baby. Your baby cries because he or she needs you—to feed or change him or her or make him or her comfortable. If you answer your baby's cry and meet your baby's needs promptly, he or she will learn there is somebody in this world who can be trusted—you. If, on the other hand, your baby's cries go unanswered and your baby's needs go unmet, he or she will learn you cannot be trusted. Babies will actually cry less often if their parents answer their cries quickly and consistently during their first 6 months or so.

Crying Rule Number Two: Your baby is definitely not trying to upset you. Your baby simply cannot figure out that crying aggravates you and your wife. The thinking skills of babies just aren't that well developed, especially before he or she is 1 year of age.

Colic Equals crazy parents

Colic is short for "about 90 days of hell!" It begins at around 2 weeks of age, hits its worst point at about 6 weeks of age, and generally goes away by the time a baby is 3 months old. In full-blown colic, the baby's abdomen feels hard and bloated ,and the child passes gas often. And the baby cries a lot.

In fact, not only will a baby with colic cry a lot, he or she also will thrash about, frantically kicking his or her legs and arms. An attack of colic usually begins in early evening and can last three to four hours. Although colic is miserable for everyone, it's not a sign of a terrible disease, bad parenting, or poor-quality breast milk. It's so common it could even be described as just a variant of normal infant development.

But all this information won't make you feel any better if you have a baby with colic. Here are some things you might try to deal with these trying times:

☛ **Talk to your pediatrician.** Unless you have other children, colic is probably a new experience for you and your wife. Ask your pediatrician to give you some advice on how to deal with it. If you have questions or concerns at 11 o'clock at night, call the doctor; that's what pediatricians are there for.

☛ **Jettison the guilt.** Remember, your baby's not crying and feeling miserable because you're doing something wrong.

☛ **Express your feelings.** Share your frustration and, yes, even your feelings of anger and inadequacy with your wife. She's feeling the same emotions. An infant is supposed to be a source of joy. But four hours of crying every night is no joy. You and your spouse need to stick together.

☛ **Try a pacifier.** No, not for you—for your baby.

☛ **Change your baby's diet.** If your baby is fed formula, talk to your pediatrician about changing the type of formula.

☛ **Get things moving.** Some babies with colic find comfort in being rocked or going for a ride in the car.

☛ **Try the colic hold.** Place your baby on his or her stomach across your knees. Then gently rub your baby's back.

☛ **Wrap up the problem.** Swaddle your baby snugly in a blanket. This works for some babies who have colic.

☛ **Make some noise.** Try pleasing sounds, such as music or a vacuum cleaner. (That's right, many babies love the noise of a vacuum.) Figure out what sounds your baby likes.

☛ **Keep those little feet warm.** Make sure your baby's feet stay covered with a warm pair of socks. Many parents swear by this trick.

☛ **Be patient.** No matter what you do, you can't cure colic. It just runs its course.

☛ **Don't label your baby.** Remember that colic has nothing to do with temperament. A baby can be easy-going and happy except when struck by an attack of colic. And, once colic has run its course, a baby can be happy and engaging or timid and irritable.

The Importance of Temperament

Babies are born with different personalities, what psychologists refer to as temperament. Some babies are easy-going and love to be cuddled. These babies may be quite happy to be still and quiet. Other babies are cautious at first and slow to warm up to new situations and people. Still other babies can be irritable. Sometimes babies are active. These are the ones that did a lot of kicking even before they were born.

The temperament with which your baby is born will influence your relationship with your child. For example, babies that are easy-going from the beginning can make their parents feel like great successes. Babies with a more difficult temperament from birth can make their parents feel like failures.

Here's something to always keep in mind: Babies simply do not choose the temperament with which they are born. It is your job as a father to come to understand your child's temperament. It's up to you to adjust your parenting style to meet your baby's needs.

You'll have to adjust your own expectations as well. An irritable baby doesn't mean you and your wife are doing something wrong. (Of course, if your baby seems to be unusually irritable, give your pediatrician a call.)

Richard Megar and daughter Andrea, 1959

=========

We don't want any of you guys thinking there's anything easy about bringing home a baby, even an "easy" baby.
Our firstborn was an "easy" baby, and I clearly remember being exhausted from sleepless nights when the only way that Jeremy would go to sleep was if Dad—and only Dad!—walked (not sat or lay down, but walked!) with him on Dad's shoulder. Once Jeremy fell asleep, I couldn't put him down in his crib or he'd wake up screaming. I remember many nights sleeping sitting up on the couch with a baby on my shoulder. And that was an "easy" baby! (JR)

=========

Babies who are slow to warm up emotionally need parents with even more patience. If you have a slow-to-warm-up baby, you'll want to allow your child time to adjust to new situations. That's the best way to help your child be comfortable and reasonably happy.

You don't want to be too pushy or energetic around a slow-to-warm-up baby; they hate that.

And you'll need to control pushy relatives, friends, or even strangers that rush up to you in the mall eager to gush over your beautiful new baby.

If you see someone being pushy, too quick to pick up your child, or just annoyingly in your baby's face, politely—but firmly— explain that that's not the kind of behavior your baby appreciates.

If your baby has a difficult temperament, you and your wife need to discuss it and support each other in dealing with it.

Your wife might not say anything, but it's likely that if she has been spending all her days with an irritable baby, she's feeling as if she's a failure as a mother. She's not a failure. She is just dealing with a difficult temperament. Make sure you help your wife understand that. You can help most of all by being really patient yourself and by setting a good example.

Whatever the temperament of your newborn, you and your wife need to stay sensitive to each other's feelings. You'll both be exhausted and, at times, frustrated.

Give each other breaks. Find time between feedings and diaper changes to say a few supportive, kind words to each other. And, although your wife will not physically be ready to have sex for several weeks after birth (and perhaps longer), find time to go to bed together and enjoy the physical and emotional comfort of each other. Trust us: She'll appreciate the hugs.

One decision a lot of families have to face is whether or not to invite someone, usually the wife's mother (yikes!), to move in for the first couple of weeks to help out.

New fathers often are surprised to learn their wives may not want anyone staying at their home after the baby is born. Women often want to prove to themselves that they have the right stuff to be a competent mother. This is difficult to do when their own mother is there taking care of things. Sometimes new mothers simply don't want to divide their attention with anyone other than their baby and husband. Other wives welcome the help, especially if this is not their first child. The obvious rule of thumb is to ask your wife what she wants to do; then do it (as usual!).

Shortly after the birth of our first daughter, *we thought a great way to get a break was to ask one of our friends to stop over and baby-sit for a few hours while we went shopping. Our friend agreed and off we went to the grocery store. About halfway down the frozen food aisle, my wife suddenly gasped, "There's something terribly wrong!" Without a moment's hesitation, she was running toward the car, leaving me with a half-full shopping cart and holding a rapidly melting container of ice cream. Arriving back home, she burst through the door only to learn our newborn had been sleeping for the now nearly 10 minutes we had been gone. (WH)*

Sleeping and Eating

Believe it or not, babies don't spend their entire newborn period crying. In fact, newborns spend most of their time sleeping. (You won't, of course, but your baby will.)

Although a newborn's first sleep may appear somewhat restless—they occasionally jerk or cough up mucus—it is usually quite deep. Even a loud noise may not awaken them. Throughout the newborn period, babies will sleep about 16 out of every 24 hours. Unfortunately for you, they package this 16 hours into 7 to 10 "naps," few of which last more than a couple of hours.

You'll probably start to feel a little paranoid about sleep—your own, that is. It will seem as though your quietly sleeping baby is programmed to feel that minuscule air motion caused by the closing of one of your eyelids, at which time he or she will wake up screaming. So, if you want to get some sleep, well, too late now, Buddy.

Babies also spend a lot of time eating. In fact, eating is closely tied to a baby's sleeping pattern. Typically, babies will sleep, wake up hungry, eat, look around a bit at all the funny new sights (most especially you), cry some, become drowsy, and fall asleep again (if you're lucky).

Your pattern will be like this: Feed the baby, play with the baby, change the baby, try to quiet the baby, give a quick thank you to God when the baby finally falls asleep, hang out with your wife, become drowsy, and ... jump when the baby cries again.

One interesting thing about babies is that, when eating, they can swallow about three times faster than an adult and can breathe at the same time they are sucking. If you tried this, you would choke.

Experts used to advise that babies be placed on feeding schedules, usually every four hours regardless of whether or not the baby appeared to be hungry. Parents were even advised to wake the baby to keep him or her on this four-hour feeding schedule. (Can you imagine anything more insane than waking your sleeping baby?)

The truth is babies will—and should be allowed to—establish their own feeding schedule. That schedule is likely to be once every three hours during the newborn period. It won't be until your baby is about 10 months old that he or she will begin eating on a three-meal-a-day schedule.

Talented from The Word "Go"

Experts also used to believe that babies were pathetic creatures who experienced the world as a "blooming, buzzing confusion." We now know that babies come into the world with a wide variety of skills and sensory capacities. Newborns will, for example, turn their head when the side of their mouth or cheek is brushed slightly to see if there is a breast or a bottle there.

Also, although they cannot see for any great distance, infants can see objects that are 7½ to 10 inches away fairly well, which is about the distance from an infant being held to a parent's face. This helps babies focus on the most important new sight since emerging from the womb—the face of their mom or dad feeding them.

Newborns also can hear. In fact, their ears have been working pretty well since about four months before they were even born. Newborns are especially responsive to sounds at 200 to 500 cycles per second, which just happens to be the frequency of the human voice. So once again, these amazing creatures seem to be hardwired to pay attention to their parents.

Babies also hear best when the sound has exaggerated changes in pitch and intonation, which is the way most adults, and even children, instinctively talk to babies. If you took our advice in Chapter 2 and talked to your baby while he or she was still in your wife's womb, your baby will be even more responsive to the sound of your voice and will be soothed and quieted by it. If not, you have some catching up to do.

Babies also have an amazingly keen sense of smell. They seem especially responsive to the smell of bananas, butter, vanilla, chocolate, honey, and strawberries. Most of all, they like the smell of their own mother's milk. This is why after a few weeks, if your wife is breast-feeding, they will turn toward her breast without even seeing.

Rather than having to develop a taste for sweets, babies are born with a sweet tooth. This predisposes a baby to like the taste of mother's milk, which is high in sugar content. It's also why hospitals sometimes feed babies sugar water during the first few days after birth if they are not taking in enough liquid. In contrast, babies hate the taste of anything sour or bitter.

Breast-Feeding

Breast-feeding is highly recommended, although far from necessary to raise a healthy baby. Many of today's adults were bottle-fed. And most of us, with the exception of crooks and politicians, seem to have turned out OK.

But breast milk does offer a few benefits formula cannot. First, breast-feeding supplies your baby with your wife's antibodies, helping to protect him or her from infections. Second, breast milk provides more healthy fats, cholesterol, protein, and iron than formula. And, breast-feeding is a special time for mother and baby.

It's not unusual for breast-feeding to take a bit of work at first. That's why doctors sometimes refer women who want to breast-feed their babies to a lactation consultant.

If your wife is breast-feeding, you need to bring a good deal of patience and understanding into this picture. Your baby may have trouble latching on to your wife's nipple on the first few attempts, even for the first couple of days. When this happens, your baby may get frustrated and do lots of screaming. As the baby's dad, you may feel tempted to rush in with a bottle, suggesting that, perhaps breast-feeding wasn't such a great idea after all. Don't. Encourage your wife to stick to it—as long as she's comfortable—and remind her that initial difficulty with breast-feeding is normal.

Besides, you can always supplement breast-feeding with a bit of dextrose or glucose water provided by the hospital during the first couple of days. (Check with your pediatrician.)

It may take some work at first, but within a few days, which can seem interminably long when dealing with a newborn, your wife and baby should be doing just fine.

Many parents worry that their newborn is not getting enough nourishment, particularly if their baby does not readily take to the breast. You and your wife should realize that many newborns do not show an interest in the breast until well after their mother begins to produce milk. This generally does not happen until two to three days after birth. Until then, the newborn feeds on a calorie- and protein-rich premilk known as colostrum. And, what is most important to keep in mind, a baby's nutritional needs at the early stages are really small.

It's also important to keep in mind that not all women can breast-feed.

It's not even all that unusual for a woman to be able to breast-feed after the birth of one child but not after another. Sometimes women don't produce enough milk. This is nothing to worry about. Doctors assure us that infant formula is healthy.

Baby Reflexes

Reflex	What it is
Rooting reflex	A tendency to turn the head in the direction of any object that gently brushes against the corner of the mouth. This reflex is most likely to show up at about a week or two of age when your baby is awake and quiet. Helps your baby find either bottle or mother's breast. Resist the temptation to tease your child with this reflex, unless you want to be awakened five times during the night instead of three!
Grasping reflex	Your baby will grasp your finger (or any other object) that is placed in the palm of his or her hand. In some cases, the grasp is so strong, you can actually lift your baby up by it. But don't! This grasping reflex disappears by the time your baby is 3 months old, after which your baby will quickly develop the ability to grasp things voluntarily.
Walking movements	If you hold your baby under the arms while gently lowering him or her to a hard surface, your baby may straighten out both legs at the knees as if trying to stand. If you then move your baby forward a bit, he or she may make stepping movements as if trying to walk. This reflex has no known practical use, but it makes for interesting conversation when guests come over to visit.
Startle reaction (or Moro reflex)	When a baby feels unsupported, even for a moment, or is exposed to a sudden, loud noise, he or she will hyperextend his or her arms and legs. At the same time, he or she will jerk the head back, then quickly bring the arms back together. This reflex, although involuntary, is your baby's way of communicating that you should be more careful in how you are handling him or her. This reflex is common between the ages of 1 and 4 months.

Note: Baby reflexes generally disappear by 3 to 4 months of age. If they do not, it could be an early indicator that something is wrong with a baby's development. If these reflexes continue past 4 months of age, discuss this with your pediatrician.

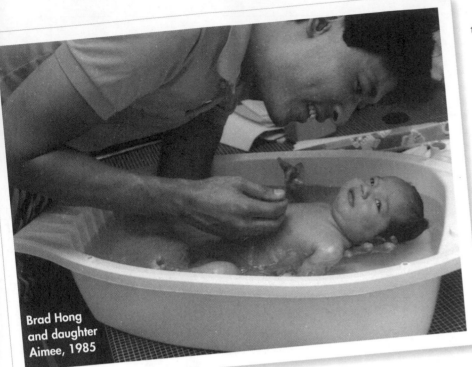

Brad Hong
and daughter
Aimee, 1985

the tough newborn stage.

Don't wait for your wife to invite you to participate. Men often are reticent to hold or feed babies because they assume their wives naturally know how to take care of a newborn. This may come as a great surprise, but our wives don't. They're just better at asking for directions. That's why our wives buy so many baby books. (Your wife is probably the one who bought you this one!)

Guys don't like to stop and ask directions. But when it comes to something as important as being a father, you should. That's what this book is all about—even if you do read it late at night … under the covers … with a flashlight. So here are some "guy" tips for surviving the newborn period.

If she can't breast-feed, your wife may feel as if she's missing out on some kind of special bonding opportunity. But trust us, your new life is now filled with magical baby moments, soon to become magical child moments, soon to become magical adolescent moments. Oops, got a little carried away there!

There's one more thing you need to be aware of: When it comes to newborns, men don't take to parenting as readily as women do. For nine months, your wife's body and mind have been preparing for a baby. Let's face it. You haven't been prepared in quite the same way.

The first couple of weeks with a baby can be intimidating to a man. You may well feel this way yourself, but don't withdraw. Don't let yourself use work as a haven from the chaos that has engulfed your home. No matter how much you normally hate dragging yourself into the workplace, you'll be tempted to focus on work and let your wife focus on the baby and home. Please don't. You started being a great father while your wife was pregnant. You need to continue being a great father during

Tips for Holding A Newborn

Hold your newborn close to your chest. Your newborn likes to hear your heartbeat. The sound reminds the little one of being in your wife's womb.

☞ **Keep the head up, please.** There will be plenty of time later for swinging your kid upside down, from side to side, and between your legs. For now, you need to be sure to support your child's head until his or her neck muscles get stronger. Whenever you pick up your baby, be sure you have one hand behind the back of your baby's head.

☞ **Let your baby see your face.** Hold your baby so he or she can look at your face. Babies love to study faces, especially the faces of Mom and Dad. The best position is to cradle your baby in your arms, face pointing up toward yours, with your baby's body almost horizontal to the ground. Your baby's head should be held slightly higher than his or her feet and snug against your body.

☛ **Don't shake the baby!** Babies can be frustrating, especially when you are tired and the baby doesn't seem to want to quiet down, no matter what you do.

Out of frustration, some parents shake their babies. This can be dangerous; it can lead to brain damage or even death. If you find yourself getting too upset, leave the baby be, even if your baby is still crying. Your baby will survive a crying spell; he or she may not survive a shaking.

Tips for Getting a Newborn to Sleep

Gently rock your baby. If this works, your baby has an easy-going temperament. Thank your lucky stars. But don't brag about it to other parents of newborns. They just might hit you.

☛ **Take your baby for a ride in the car.** This trick is an old stand-by. The only trouble is that when you stop the car, your baby often wakes and starts crying again. It's also hard on the gasoline budget, which is why President Jimmy Carter tried to ban this parenting practice during the mid-'70s gasoline shortage.

☛ **Vacuum the floor.** We're not kidding—it works. The vacuum generates a constant white noise, which seems to have a soothing effect on babies. And your wife will appreciate the sparkling clean rug.

☛ **Don't overstimulate your baby during the day.** Some parents believe they should stimulate their babies during the day so they will sleep better at night. Actually, the opposite is true. When your baby is quiet and content, don't overstimulate him or her, unless, of course, you enjoy being stimulated yourself by a screaming baby at 2 or 3 o'clock in the morning.

☛ **Put a ticking clock in your baby's crib.** Some people swear this quiets a baby. The ticking sound supposedly resembles the sound of your wife's heartbeat, the soothing sound your baby heard while still in the womb.

☛ **Turn up the volume slowly.** Especially for the first few days at home with your newborn, you should keep the house quieter and darker than usual. This helps your baby adjust to his or her new and noisier environment. But don't feel you have to keep the house as quiet as a chapel during nap time. Indeed, after a couple of weeks, you don't want to. If you do, as your child gets older, he or she may wake up at the sound of any noise.

Tips for Keeping Your Marriage Together

Talk with each other. Before your baby was born, you each had a good deal of independence. You came and went as you pleased and kept to your own schedules. Each of you was, in many ways, a free agent. All of this has now changed. No parent fully appreciates just how much change having a baby brings. Your only hope for sanity is to remember that you and your wife are a team.

☛ **Keep the romance alive.** Most of your waking hours will be fixated on satisfying the needs of this tiny creature you voluntarily (what were you thinking!) brought into this world. When your baby is all changed, fed, and asleep, it will be hard to think of anything but getting some shut-eye yourself. But remember: There's someone else who needs your attention. In fact, she's even more exhausted than you. So snuggle up to her and go comatose together, and life will be far easier. Ignore her, and welcome to Nightmare on Elm Street.

A good start is to surprise her with a candlelight dinner and champagne during your baby's first week at home. The meal doesn't have to be elaborate, even a microwaved frozen dinner will do the trick. Sparkling cider should be substituted for the champagne if your wife is breast-feeding.

It's worth repeating that parents who are happily married are more likely to have children who are emotionally healthier than are parents who are not happy in their marriage. Remember, your child's emotional health is extremely important. Yours is, too. Don't take your marriage for granted. It's not good for you, your wife, or your child.

☛ **Be prepared for your wife's postpartum blues.** Following the birth of your baby, your wife may experience a period of moodiness caused by changes in hormonal levels (or the sudden appearance of her mother-in-law at the doorstep).

During this time, your wife may feel anxious or depressed, believing that she is not being a good mother, that your baby has some deadly disease, or that you don't love her anymore. Or, she may feel blue for no identifiable reason.

This moodiness is often troubling for fathers who can't understand why their wives would feel this way. It is important to know that these feelings are common and usually pass, especially if you are supportive and reassuring.

If these feelings persist or become intense, your wife might want to talk the situation over with her ob-gyn, who will be able to tell if it requires professional attention.

My wife's form of postpartum blues was to fret continuously over the health of our firstborn. *One afternoon, my wife became convinced our daughter was developing a fever. Upon remembering I had driven our only car to work that morning, she frantically ran out into the street, hailed a taxi, and rushed our daughter to the pediatrician—where the baby was pronounced perfectly fine. It was only after she arrived back home via another (expensive) taxi ride that she discovered I had left our car parked on the street in front of the house just in case she needed it. It was 10 years before she had the nerve to tell me about this. (WH)*

☛ **Be prepared for postpartum blues.** Believe it or not, men also can suffer from postpartum blues. Most commonly, a man's blues are related either to feeling left out because of the amount of attention his wife is giving to their newborn or to worries about being able to provide adequately for his now larger family.

The key to avoiding postpartum blues is for fathers to get involved right away with the care of their newborn. It also helps to get some rest (yeah, right) and take occasional breaks from parenting, even if only for an hour or two, with either your wife or other new dads with whom you can swap fatherhood "war stories."

☛ **Enjoy the moment.** Soon, something will happen that will make all the exhaustion that the two of you are experiencing seem worthwhile. Your baby's tiny lips will turn up spontaneously in a smile when he or she is drowsy or sleeping. Experts used to say this smile was due to gas. Now they're not so sure what causes newborns to smile. We are. Your baby is smiling at you.

the first
year
of life

Whew! Those first few weeks are finally over and you're gaining confidence as a dad.

You're well on your way to mastering the five B's of baby care: bathing, bottles, burping, bottoms, and bonding. Now you can relax.

Well … not exactly. Over the course of the next year, your life will go through countless adaptations as you come to realize this incredible truth: This baby has taken over your life!

So, what do you do now? Lots. Let's start with the basics.

Grandpa Howard Weintraub, son Brent, and grandson Jared, 1997

Eagle's Eye View of your baby's first year

During the first year of life, your baby will make an extraordinary number of developmental advances. Your baby will go from crying to using a few words and from not being able to hold up his or her own head to a skilled crawler who might be taking his or her first tentative steps.

By the age of 1 year, your child will have developed a love for play and the capacity for solving simple problems. The amount of development that you are about to witness over the next 12 months is simply amazing. Pay attention. You don't want to miss any of it.

Age in months	Motor development	Language and communication development
Newborn	Limbs and body move in response to sudden changes, such as noise. Moves head side-to-side when on back.	Cries.
1	Can raise head while on stomach.	Responds to and usually is soothed by others' voices. Cries for help.
2	Can move arms; swipes at objects. Can raise head up and hold it up for short time while lying on stomach.	Can tell the difference between some sounds. Makes cooing sounds.
3	Can lift up head and chest when lying facedown. Reaches for and grasps objects.	Makes cooing sounds. Says short words, such as "ga." Laughs. Will turn head when he or she hears a voice.
4	Can turn head when lying down or seated. Grasps small objects placed in hand.	Babbles in strings of baby sounds, such as "gagaga." Smiles at the person speaking to him or her.
5	Sits supported for up to 30 minutes. Rolls from stomach to back. If pulled up by the hands, can stand with support.	Can tell the difference between angry and friendly voices. Imitates some sounds. Will respond to his or her name.
6	Turns head freely. Can sit up straight if lightly supported by a chair. Holds bottle. Creeps.	Can let you know if happy or unhappy using volume and assorted baby sounds. Squeals when excited.
7	Pushes up to hands and knees. Can eat some strained solid foods. Easily transfers objects from hand to hand.	Plays at making different sounds. Begins to look at some objects when they are named.
8	Crawls. Grabs furniture and pulls up to a standing position. Needs help to get back down.	Recognizes some words. Imitates gestures and tones of adult speech.
9	Can stand alone for a brief time and can get back down from a standing position by himself or herself. Sits without support. Can move to sitting position then to crawling position without help.	Begins to make strings of babbling sounds that have the sound patterns of adult speech. Uses gestures for communication.
10	Crawls well. Holds and drinks from a baby cup.	Can obey some commands. Imitates some adult speech.
11	Can stand by himself or herself. Climbs up stairs. Feeds self with a spoon.	Imitates rhythms, sounds, and facial expressions of adults.
12	Can take first steps by himself or herself, or while holding an adult's hand. Can use a spoon, cup, and crayons or pencils.	Recognizes his or her own name. Understands "no." Can follow simple instructions such as "Say bye-bye." Says his or her first real word, such as "DaDa," "MaMa," or "bye-bye."

Expect Changes in Your Life

You, too, will be changing a lot during the first year of your baby's life. Before you became a father, your life was more or less your own. You could (with your wife's consent, of course) work late at the office or go work out at the gym.

You could go out with the guys or just sit at home and watch TV. You could have sex whenever you and your wife wanted, and you could sleep late on weekends. Now you can't do any of those things. You have a brand-new person to consider.

Men frequently react to the financial pressure of having started a family by working longer and harder. Some volunteer for lots of overtime. Others take on second jobs. Most of all, fathers worry a lot about money.

But becoming preoccupied with financial concerns can have two unfortunate results. First, it can cause your wife to believe you have abandoned her, leaving her to care for your little one all by herself. Second, you will be missing out on one of the best—and most important—years of fatherhood.

Some dads don't believe they have much to offer an infant except their ability to earn money. They assume that early nurturing is mostly women's work and await the arrival of soccer games and Little League to get involved in their kids' lives. Wrong approach.

Your child needs your involvement early and frequently. In fact, studies show that fathers who are actively engaged with their babies in the first year of life rear more successful children. One study by J. Kevin Nugent, Ph.D., director of the Brazelton Institute at Harvard Medical School, for example, found that fathers who regularly talked to, played with, soothed, and fed their babies during the first few months of life had children who had more advanced motor, word recognition, and problem-solving skills at age 1 year.

Babies who spend a great deal of time with their fathers also have been found to be more sociable, affectionate, and verbal. Yet, one study found that, on average, fathers spend

Dan Benshoff with daughters Emma Jane and Olivia, 1996

only 37 seconds a day with their infants in warm voice interactions, such as cooing and laughing. Thirty-seven seconds a day! These men are building a better relationship with their television remote control.

The good news is that fathers are becoming more involved in the daily rearing of their children. According to one national poll, 84 percent of men report spending more time with their children and performing more household duties than their own fathers did.

This is not just the men's opinions. Research done by Joseph H. Pleck, Ph.D., professor of human development and family studies at the University of Illinois at Urbana-Champaign, has documented that fathers are spending 50 percent more time interacting with their kids and doing household tasks than did fathers just a generation ago.

Still, men spend less time than women caring for children. To some extent, this is to be expected. Unless

Back to Work

If you're lucky, you have been able to arrange for an extended period of paternity leave. Or, perhaps you'll take our advice and cobble together several weeks (even several months) of vacation and sick time in order to be with your wife and baby. But no matter what you do, no matter how many excuses you come up with, sooner or later you will have to go back to work. See, babies may be small but they are voracious consumers. In plain English, that baby of yours is going to cost a lot of money.

Here, based on information from the U.S. Department of Agriculture, is a handy chart to help you understand just how much this baby is going to cost over his or her childhood (please sit down before reading it).

A family earning:	Will spend this much before their child graduates from high school:	Upon recognizing this fact, the father will:
$21,600 a year	$178,080*	Scream
$46,100 a year	$241,440*	Weep
$87,300 a year	$350,920*	Demand a bigger tax deduction

* Does not include cost of college tuition.

your last name is Rockefeller, someone has to work outside the home during the first year of a child's life and that someone usually is the father. When a dad works outside the home and the mom stays home with the baby, it just follows that the mom will do more of the daily child care.

It doesn't have to be that way, of course. Some dads do stay home while their wives work outside the home. Other couples work split shifts so that at least one of the parents can always be home with the baby.

In fact, according to the U.S. Census Bureau, nearly one in five fathers is the primary child care provider when mothers of preschoolers work outside the home. But mother at home and father in the workplace is still the most common arrangement for much of the first year of a child's life.

However you and your wife make things work this first year, you should understand that working outside the home is not an excuse for performing few, if any, child care duties. Nobody said that working and raising a family would be easy. And raising children well is definitely a joint undertaking. So you are just going to have

to make some adjustments to your schedule to make sure you fulfill your responsibilities as a father as well as an economic provider.

In fact, your child's development will suffer if you are away from home too much. A study done at the University of California at Berkeley found that 3-year-olds whose fathers worked more than 40 hours a week outside the home were more anxious, less warm, and less adept at such cognitive tasks as role-playing and object classification (important early thinking skills) compared to children whose fathers worked outside the home 40 hours or less a week.

Spending time with your baby helps him or her develop well and strengthens your confidence in being a dad. Breast-feeding is out of the question for you (oh, gee, I needed a book to tell me that!), but there are lots of other things you can do with your baby:

☛ **Play with your baby.**

☛ **Burp your baby after a feeding.**

☛ **Change your baby's diapers.**

☛ **Take your baby out into the neighborhood in a carriage or stroller.**

- **Rock your baby to sleep.**
- **Sing to your baby.**
- **Read a book to your baby.** (Don't worry about whether your baby can understand the story.)

Married with Children

Some changes are in order if your marriage is to survive children. First, you and your wife are going to have to accept and come to appreciate the following truth: When it comes to parenting, fathers and mothers do it differently.

From the beginning of a child's life, dads tend to be more physical in their interaction with their kids, whereas moms are more verbal. Dads also tend to be more encouraging of independence, achievement, and risk-taking; moms are more encouraging of closeness to the family, caution, and safety. In addition, dads tend to exert greater control over their children, and moms are more sensitive to their emotional needs. It is not that one way of parenting is better than the other, only that they are different.

Experts now agree that children do best when they are exposed to the different and often complementary behavior of both mothers and fathers. That is, children need both verbal and physical stimulation, along with encouragement to take risks and to exercise caution, as well as discipline and affectionate support.

It would be absurd to suggest that mothers and fathers should be so highly specialized there is no overlap between their parenting behaviors.

Of course, fathers should be nurturers as well as disciplinarians, and mothers should be disciplinarians as well as nurturers. And both are perfectly capable of roughhousing with their children as well as reading them bedtime stories.

But the fact remains that, on average, mothers and fathers parent differently, and this is a good thing. For in the words of James Levine, Ed.D., director of The

Making Time
for your infant

This is not the time for excuses. Now is the time to make yourself available to your child. You might as well get in the habit. It's something you're going to be doing for the next couple of decades. Here are some places to find those extra hours:

- **Sacrifice one leisure activity.** Instead of perfecting your tennis serve, perfect the art of burping.
- **Trade at least one solitary activity for one family activity.** Replace golf with family hikes in the park.
- **Readjust your spending habits.** Eat out less frequently, for instance, or spend less money on your golf game, so you can spend more time at home.
- **Negotiate creative work arrangements with your employer.** If your work involves staring at a computer screen all day, see if your employer will allow you to telecommute from home, either full-time or part-time. Or, see about rearranging your work schedule so you can be at home at least part of one day each week so your wife can run errands, work outside the home herself, or just take some time off from baby duty.
- **Take work home instead of working overtime at the office.** When you are working at home, at least you are accessible to your kids. Try to make working late at the office more the exception than the rule.

Fatherhood Project of the Families and Work Institute, "A child who is highly involved with both parents has a rich emotional palette from which to draw." Learn this, and you will save your marriage from a lot of arguments about who is doing it "right."

Early in your child's life, you and your wife also need to come to understand and appreciate the different ways men and women react to the stress of having a

Mars & Venus
in the nursery

When Mom's and Dad's unique parenting styles are both in play, the equation works out quite nicely:

Dad	Mom
Physical	Verbal
Encourages independence, achievement, and risk-taking	Encourages family closeness, caution, and safety

+

Control	Sensitivity

=

A Great Parenting Team!

baby in the house. According to psychologist Jay Belsky, Ph.D., professor of human development at Pennsylvania State University, husbands often feel resentful of their wive's seemingly obsessive preoccupation with the baby and react angrily to how little affection and attention their wives seem to have left over for them. Wives, by contrast, frequently become upset at what they perceive as their husbands' preoccupation with their own emotional needs.

Moreover, men frequently react to the financial pressures associated with a baby by becoming more frugal, whereas women more freely spend money to ensure the baby's well-being.

Here's a prescription for keeping your marriage strong under the stress of a baby:

☞ **Talk, don't argue.** Spend a lot of time talking to each other about what you have in common, rather than arguing about your differences.

☞ **Communicate parental feelings.** Spend time sharing how much each of you loves your baby.

☞ **Plan future memories.** Work at creating new family traditions for your brand-new family.

☞ **Determine how household chores are going to get done.** The point here is not to negotiate a 50–50 split for getting chores done. What really matters is that each person is seen by the other as contributing significantly to the care and upkeep of both the baby and the home.

☞ **Don't sulk in silence.** If hurt feelings do start to build, talk about them with each other in a nonjudgmental way. Lingering resentments can create real trouble for a marriage. If you see this happening in your marriage, it may be time to seek professional help.

The key is to communicate, communicate, communicate. Don't let little resentments build.

☞ **Honor your spouse.** Work at appreciating the different contributions each of you makes to the well-being of your family.

Sex after Baby

Remember sex? That's what you and your wife used to do when you were alone together and had extra time on your hands. Now all you seem to be doing is running around taking care of your baby's needs. What about your needs?

The good news is that there is sex after a baby—eventually. Although many women experience pain during intercourse following childbirth, especially if they have had an episiotomy, the pain usually disappears after several weeks.

Breast-feeding can cause a thinning of the vaginal tissue as well as dryness that can make intercourse uncomfortable for your wife. The rule of thumb: If it's painful for your wife, don't do it. If the pain continues past the second month after birth, however, your wife may want to consult her doctor.

In addition to possible physical discomfort, fatigue and other psychological factors, such as the intense bonding between your wife and the baby, may interfere with your wife's sexual desire. Don't be too alarmed by this. It is perfectly natural, and with time, sexual desire almost always returns.

In the meantime, you may want to substitute physical closeness and emotional intimacy for sexual intercourse. In fact, the worst thing you can do is to exert pressure on your wife to resume sexual relations before she is ready to do so.

Many couples get used to unprotected sex during pregnancy and either "forget" to resume birth control or don't take into account some important changes. But, unless you're eager to give your baby a brand-new brother or sister, you're going to have to be careful.

Your wife will need to discuss possible changes in her preferred method of birth control with her doctor. If your wife had been using a diaphragm, for example, it may no longer fit snugly as a result of the stretching that occurred to the cervix during childbirth. If your wife is breast-feeding, she will have to avoid birth control pills that contain estrogen, since it can effect lactation.

Barrier methods, such as diaphragms and condoms, are reasonably effective and will not interfere with milk production. More drastic birth control measures include vasectomy and tubal ligation, but you should be absolutely sure you do not want any additional children before using these methods.

Helping Your Baby Grow Up Healthy

For your child to grow up healthy, happy, and secure, you have to continually make sure that your child:
- is physically healthy
- is emotionally healthy and self-confident
- develops good cognitive and language skills
- learns to control his or her behavior

Tough assignment. Fortunately, you're not the first dad in the history of humankind. There is an accumulated body of knowledge that can help you. Some has been discovered by social scientists. A lot of it comes from ordinary human experience. So let's begin.

Joe Vesselles with daughter Monica and son Jay, 1996

First, your child needs to be healthy. By now, you've undoubtedly chosen a pediatrician or family practitioner to help look after your baby's physical health. If you haven't yet taken this important step, it's time to get moving. To stay healthy, your child will need regular medical checkups.

The first checkup should take place one to two weeks after birth. The doctor will usually want to see your child every two months after that until he or she is 6 months old, then every three months until your child's first birthday.

Your child's doctor will also want to see your child at least two more times between the ages of 1 and 2 years.

To keep your child healthy, you will also have to make sure your home is a safe place to be a baby.

Here are some suggestions:

☞ **Don't smoke around your baby.** Don't let anybody else smoke around your child either.

Breathing secondhand smoke can cause ear and lung infections in children and can make children's respiratory diseases, such as asthma, worse. And it certainly doesn't help to smoke in one room while your child is in another room. If you must smoke, do it outside.

☞ **Always use an approved infant car seat.** You will be tempted sometimes, especially on short car trips, to have someone hold your baby instead of using the infant car seat.

You should be aware that most car accidents occur within only a few miles of the home. A few minutes spent making sure your child is always strapped in is one of the best tragedy prevention habits you will ever develop.

☞ **Childproof your home.** Each year, some 415,000 children 1 year of age and younger are exposed to something poisonous, and 35,000 children are injured seriously enough to warrant medical attention.

Fortunately, there are a number of things that you can do to make your home a safe place for your baby to crawl around:

- **Cover up all electrical outlets.**
- **Don't leave small objects anywhere near where small hands can reach them.**
- **Put locks on all your cabinets, especially in the kitchen and bathrooms.**
- **Remember that a baby's instinct is to put any new object in his or her mouth.**
- **Put all poisons out of reach.**

It is surprising to learn how common household substances can be deadly to babies, who have been known to die from ingesting large quantities of caffeine pills, mouthwash, meat tenderizers, seasoning salts, and especially iron supplements. In fact, iron overdose is the most common cause of pediatric

death by poisoning. So if it's not baby food, keep it out of reach.

═══════

We learned about the potential danger of poisoning the hard way. *We were distracted by cleaning up the house, when our 15-month-old daughter crawled up onto the kitchen counter (something she had never done before) and drank a bottle of cold medicine. Forcing my child to take syrup of ipecac to make her vomit is not an experience I ever wish to have again. (WH)*

═══════

Free Stuff:
for home safety

As your child ages, you'll find that he or she has the newfound ability to get into ever-increasing amounts of trouble. Periodically, conduct a childproofing tour of your home. The following free brochures are available to help you do this.

The Juvenile Products Manufacturers Association (JPMA) publishes a free booklet called *Safe & Sound for Baby*. It can be obtained by sending a stamped, self-addressed envelope to:

Juvenile Products Manufacturers Association
236 Rte. 38, West
Suite 100
Moorestown, NJ 08057

The Consumer Product Safety Commission (CPSC) has two free brochures, *Tips for Your Baby's Safety* and *The Safe Nursery*. They can be obtained by writing:

Consumer Product Safety Commission
Office of Information and Public Affairs
Washington, DC 20207

Emotional Health

Emotional health is the key to self-confidence, and self-confidence is one of the keys to succeeding at anything, whether it's school or sports. Children who are emotionally healthy and self-confident understand that tasks can be difficult, but will still want to try out new activities. They can accept frustration and try several times to complete a new or different task. Because emotionally healthy children also feel secure in trying out new relationships, they are more likely to develop good social skills. They will know how to get along with adults and other children.

The foundation for emotional healt_ laid in the first year of life through the bal_ relationship with his or her parents. T_ relationship is called attachment. Childr_ who have developed a secure attachme_ feel they are safe to explore the world ar_ to relate to a growing number of peopl_ outside the family.

Experts used to believe that a baby's strongest attachment was to his or her mother. However, research shows that when fathers are actively involved in the care of their infants, babies become just as strongly attached to their fathers. Here are some suggestions for helping your infant build a strong attachment to you:

☛ **Spend time with your baby.** important way you can help your baby develop a secure attachment to you is to interact with him or her on a regular basis.

☛ **Respond to your baby's needs.** One-year-olds who are securely attached have parents who were responsive to their cries, smiles, and other signals when they were babies. If you answer your baby's cries and meet your baby's needs quickly, he

or she will learn that you can be trusted. As an added payoff, babies will cry less often if their parents answer their cries in a timely manner, especially during the first three months after birth. If, on the other hand, your baby's cries go unanswered and needs go unmet, your baby will learn that the world is an unsafe, untrustworthy place.

☛ **Be affectionate.** Parents who are sensitive and warm toward their babies have been found to have babies who are securely attached.

☛ **Have fun with your baby.** By 3 months of age, your baby will have developed a social smile that indicates when he or she is happy. If you spend a lot of time playing with your

Jon Hoogensen and son Jacob, 1995

frequently bring a smile to your baby's face. Be honest: How many other people smile as soon as they see you?

☛ **Don't withdraw from or force yourself on your baby.** It is not uncommon for infants between the ages of 6 and 12 months to have a preference for their moms, especially if Mom is the one who stays home with the baby while Dad goes to work. When this happens, it is natural for the dad to feel offended or jealous. This can lead to either withdrawal or stubborn insistence on interacting with the baby. Either reaction will only make things worse. Instead, be patient and

Kevin Oberman and daughter Galya, 1997

look for opportunities to interact with your baby when he or she is relaxed. (And take comfort in the fact that today's rejected parent may be tomorrow's favorite.)

☛ **Attend to your marriage.** Parents who are happily married are more likely to have children who are securely attached than are parents who are not satisfied with their marriage. It is especially important that you and your wife find time to be alone together.

Arrange for a baby-sitter you trust, such as a friend, a relative, or a neighbor, and start taking short outings away from home and the baby. To help manage any anxiety you or your wife may feel about leaving your little one with someone else, be sure to leave phone numbers with the baby-sitter where you can be reached and feel free to check-in yourselves.

A good goal is getting out once a week, even if it's only for a quick cup of coffee.

Helping Your Child Survive Separation

Parents are frequently concerned when their baby develops a tendency to be distressed or anxious whenever separated for a short time from his or her parents. This tendency is often accompanied by anxiety around strangers.

These fearful moments usually begin between the ages of 6 and 7 months. They are perfectly normal. In fact, both indicate that a child has developed a good attachment with his or her parents and has attained an important cognitive skill called object permanence— basically, the realization that when objects, such as Mom and Dad, are out of sight, they still exist somewhere in the universe.

Here's how you can help:

☛ **Reassure your baby that you will be returning.** Your baby may not understand your words, but the tone of your voice may help soothe troubled emotions.

☛ **Demonstrate your affection.** Give plenty of hugs and comforting words when you do return.

☛ **Play peekaboo games.** This gives your baby practice in understanding that things that go out of sight, do return. (Bet you thought this game was just for fun!)

Many babies cope with separation distress by employing what psychologists call transitional objects. Your baby will come to call such a transitional object "blanky" or "dee dee" and rely upon it to give comfort when Mommy and Daddy are not around. The use of such transitional objects is quite normal and should not be discouraged. Indeed, a favorite blanket, pillow, or stuffed animal can be a tremendous tool for helping your child manage his or her anxiety over your absence.

My oldest daughter developed an extraordinary attachment to a fuzzy, stuffed monkey. *She brought that monkey everywhere. The neighbors became so used to seeing that monkey in my daughter's arms that they eventually dubbed it "Monkey Horn." (WH)*

Helping Your Child Cope With Stranger Anxiety

Stranger anxiety is best dealt with by gradually introducing your baby to any new person.

It is equally important to impress upon the "stranger" that he or she should not force himself or herself on your baby. If your baby has a slow-to-warm-up temperament, this may take a long time. Take comfort in the fact that these are normal baby reactions that actually indicate you are doing everything right.

Helping Your Child Learn

You will need to help your child develop what psychologists call good cognitive skills. It sounds complicated, but all it means is that you get to play a role in teaching your child how to think. In order for you to do this most effectively, we'll need to take a look at how your baby's brain develops.

At birth, a baby's brain is only about 25 percent of its eventual adult weight and size. During the first year of life, a child's brain grows quickly. By age 1 year, a child's brain is about 75 percent of its eventual adult weight and size.

Of course, children do not simply sit around and wait for their brains to grow. Children are constantly learning how to use the ever-growing power of their brain as it develops. This is called cognitive development.

Children use their eyes, ears, nose, mouth, and skin to gather information from the world. This information is processed by their brain.

Exposure to new information requires children to widen their understanding of the world: how things work, why they work, what happens if somebody does something. This gives children a broader, better understanding of how the world works. This is called learning.

Children naturally seek to understand their world. That is why children are always experimenting with everyday items, toys, even words. How complicated a child's experiments are and how much information can be processed are determined by how far along the child's brain has developed.

Getting to Know Your Baby

There are many ways you can help your baby develop cognitively. We have already talked about one. That is helping your baby form a secure attachment to you and your wife as parents.

You also can teach your child that communication is satisfying, that words are fun, and new experiences are exciting.

Here are some suggestions for things you can try:

☞ **Talk to your baby.** Parents regularly have conversations with their babies, even from birth. Most parents naturally talk to their babies in short sentences with short simple words. Parents also use voices that sound happy and facial expressions that look happy.

These are good techniques that help keep your baby interested in having conversations with you. These conversations are important. The more you talk to your baby the more your child will make baby sounds, such as cooing and babbling. These are the beginnings of speech.

☛ **Integrate your baby into the home environment.** Babies are attracted to movement and variety, so don't just leave your baby lying on his or her back staring at the ceiling all day long. Starting at between 2 and 4 weeks, place your baby in an infant seat or prop him or her up in the corner of a sofa with cushions so your baby can see what's going on around him or her.

☛ **Interact with your baby.** Colorful mobiles and toys have their place in stimulating babies, but it is even more important that you physically interact with your baby.

Spend time tickling your baby (gently!), playing peekaboo, and rubbing his or her arms and legs. Make your baby's favorite toy be you.

☛ **Read books and sing to your baby.** It is never too early to begin to read and sing to your child. Even when your child is an infant, you can sit your baby in your lap and read or sing to him or her.

For reading, choose children's books that are bright and colorful and use simple words. Babies especially like books that have lots of rhythm, melody, and repetition, such as nursery rhymes.

Babies older than 6 months also like books such as *Pat the Bunny* that encourage them to interact physically. And don't worry about finishing the book. What is most important is that the time you spend reading together is enjoyable for both you and your baby.

☛ **Be an explorer with your baby.** Point out things to your baby. Say, "Look!" when you see a dog on the street or a bird in a tree. Tell your baby it's a "dog" or a "birdie." Name objects your baby is looking at: "Ooh, it's a ball! Does Christen want the ball? Here's the ball!" As your baby grows, he or she will learn that words are an important part of the world. This is the first step toward building a good vocabulary.

Teaching Your Child "Good" Behavior

Your child also will need to develop the ability to self-regulate his or her behavior. By self-regulation, we mean the ability to delay impulses in order to follow rules.

Developing the capacity to self-regulate behavior is absolutely critical for success in life. Without this skill, your child will not be able to cooperate, take turns, or listen. In short, without the capacity for self-regulation, your child will not be able to get along with other people. Teaching your child to self-regulate his or her behavior may be one of the most important things you will do as a father.

If you had the good sense to have a daughter, teaching self-regulation is likely to be easier. In general, boys are more active and aggressive than girls. For example, boisterous wrestling is more frequently seen in boys than in girls. This isn't true for all boys and girls, but it's true much of the time. All this means is that it typically takes more time and effort to teach boys to self-regulate their behavior than it does girls. It's not impossible; it just takes longer.

═══════════

Our family is scientific proof that boys are more active. *Our twins are one of each: a boy and a girl. At 2 years old, they're both a handful, but when it comes to aggressive behavior, there's no comparison. Justin has been appropriately nicknamed "Bustin" by his older brother. His jumping about, slamming doors, and throwing anything not nailed down and less than 100 pounds, has resulted in untold dollars' worth of damage to our house, from broken picture frames to doors ripped off hinges. His twin sister may draw on walls and make a mess every chance she gets, but she's no "Bustin." (JR)*

═══════════

One way to help children develop self-regulation is to teach your child manners. Some people balk at the idea that manners are necessary because they seem so arbitrary. Why, for heaven's sake, do you have to keep your elbows off the table when eating?

Manners may be arbitrary, and they do differ from culture to culture, but they are still important. Manners require that you bring your behavior under the control of a social convention. In other words, manners require that you follow a rule. In addition, when children have good manners, other adults and children like to be around them. (This enhances a child's chances of doing well in life.)

Many people mistakenly believe you have to wait until a child is heading out the door to school before you start teaching self-regulation and good manners. In reality, what you teach your child in the first year of life helps lay the foundation for a lifetime of good behavioral health.

You can, for example, begin teaching your baby manners by using good manners yourself around your baby. This shows your baby that having respect for people and their feelings is important.

Sleeping through The Night

An important way to teach self-regulation and impulse control is helping your child learn to sleep through the night. If you're lucky, your baby will do this without any training. (Just don't go and brag about it to the parents of other infants, though; it will only aggravate them). Most babies require a little help, however.

You can begin teaching your baby to sleep through the night when the child is about 4 to 5 months of age. Keeping in mind that you will need to proceed gradually, the essential point is to help your baby differentiate between daytime and nighttime. A good first step is to keep the lights dim and the atmosphere calm during evening feedings. This helps the baby understand that evening equates with darkness and reduced activity level.

Jack Bryson and daughter Tywayah, 1971

Second, begin slowly to cut afternoon snoozes short. Third, establish an evening bedtime routine. By doing the same things every night, in roughly the same order, the bedtime routine will soon begin to signal to your baby that it is time to go to sleep.

Finally, after—and only after—you have done all of the above, you can start to allow your baby to cry just a little bit at night before going in to comfort him or her.

One method for helping your child learn how to get to sleep at night is described in Richard Ferber's book *Solve Your Child's Sleeping Problems*. It involves putting your baby in his or her crib while the little one is still awake, offering comfort for a few minutes, then leaving the room.

If your baby cries, wait approximately five minutes then go in to make sure your baby is not ill, hurt, or in need of a diaper change.

If he or she is not, spend two or three minutes soothing your baby, but do not pick your baby up. After this relatively quick comforting session, leave the room before the baby goes to sleep. (You want to teach your baby to fall asleep without you having to be around.)

If your baby continues to cry, wait a little longer this time (maybe 10 minutes) before going back in. Again, check quickly to make sure that everything is all right. You also need to spend a few minutes soothing and reassuring your baby—but do not pick him or her up.

The next time, wait 15 minutes before going back into your baby's bedroom. Continue checking every 15 minutes until your baby falls asleep.

Using this procedure four or five nights in a row usually does the trick. The key to success is consistency. Using this technique intermittently (sometimes picking up your baby, sometimes not, or using it on Monday night, but not on Tuesday) is likely to make this process more difficult.

It is important to emphasize that the Ferber method is not the same as letting kids cry themselves to sleep. It is important that you intermittently go into your baby's room to reassure both you and your baby that everything is all right.

Also, this method is not meant for every baby. Some babies are simply too fearful, particularly those who are experiencing a particularly intense period of separation anxiety, for this method to be successful.

Remember: Sleeping through the night has a different meaning for a baby than it does for adults. A baby who sleeps through the night at age 3 or 4 months is a baby who is sleeping about five hours straight—six, if you're lucky. In other words, a good sleeper is a baby who goes down at midnight and gets up to feed at 6 a.m. This is hardly what most of us would consider to be a good night's sleep!

Giving Up the Pacifier

Many, perhaps most, parents give babies pacifiers for a simple reason: They work. Indeed, the only persons who love pacifiers more than screaming babies are parents of screaming babies. Inevitably, however, one is confronted with the question: When is it time to give up the pacifier?

Medical science provides only part of the answer. Although many parents tend to worry that pacifiers can cause tooth alignment problems, up until the age of 5 years, pacifiers can't do much damage. So, as long as your child gives up the pacifier before heading off to kindergarten, medically it's probably OK. But the more important reason for having your child give up the pacifier is that it helps your child learn how to pacify himself or herself without an external aid.

Regardless of when you decide to help your child kick the pacifier habit, the key to success is going slowly. Here are our suggestions:

☛ **Lessen the pleasure.** A good first step is to slit the rubber end of the pacifier so that sucking on it is less satisfying for your baby.

☛ **Do a disappearing act.** Gradually reduce the situations where you make the pacifier available to your baby. Start with situations in which your baby is least likely to demand the pacifier, such as when your baby is playing with toys.

☛ **Know when to make exceptions.** Allow your baby access to the pacifier in situations and places where it has come to be expected, such as in the crib or in the car seat.

☛ **Buy some ear plugs.** Some parents prefer to force their child to go cold turkey. If you do, be prepared for three or four days of screaming.

the toddler and preschool years

Your sleepless nights are now beginning to reap great dividends.

You're not done with sleepless nights, not by a long shot—not until your son or daughter reaches the age of, oh, say about 25. But that little baby has become a little child, and you're getting to know the person you and your wife have created.

Your daughter's becoming Daddy's little princess (who, we hope, will also love to play baseball). And you've now learned that the female capacity for wrapping men around their little fingers with just a look is perfected by the age of 1 year.

Bill Brett and daughter Eily Ann, 1996

The Toddler Years

This chart outlines average physical and language development between the ages of 1 and 5 years. You should keep in mind that this chart shows average development. Children can be well ahead or well behind and still be within the normal range. Ask your pediatrician if you have any questions or concerns.

Age in months	Motor development	Language and communication development
15	Child is a mini hurricane, always moving. Can wave bye-bye while walking. Can throw a ball. Can take off his or her socks and shoes. Can scribble lines with a crayon.	When an adult names a nearby object, the child can point to it. This includes people, pets, and toys. Has a four- to six-word vocabulary. Of course, the child's words will not sound much like adult words. Juice might be said as "dus," baby might sound like "bibi," and doggie might sound like "doddie" or "goggie."
18	With help from an adult, can walk up and down stairs. Can drink from a cup without assistance. Can scribble in circles.	Uses first sentences. These consist of two words such as "throw ball," "doggie bed," "more cookie." Can identify a few parts of the body. Refers to himself or herself by name.
21	Walks up and down stairs by holding on to railing or adult's hand. Jumps, runs, throws, and climbs. Unzips coats and clothes. Can put together a simple puzzle with large pieces.	Uses I, me, and mine. Enjoys rhyming games. Sentences are still two words.
24 (2 years)	From a standing position, can bend down at the waist to pick something up. Walks up or down stairs with little or no help. Runs, but may fall when turning quickly. Can eat with a fork.	Can name most common, everyday objects. Uses short sentences. Many sentences are three words, such as "Eat big cookie." or "Daddy throw ball." Some sentences will be four words, such as "Me eat big cookie." or "Daddy throw big ball."
36 (3 years)	Walks without watching his or her feet. Rides a tricycle. Can draw pictures that represent something.	Regularly uses three- or four-word sentences. Can follow two-step commands, such as "Go to your room and pick up your car." Often asks "what?" and "where?"
48 (4 years)	Walks up and down stairs smoothly, alternating steps as older children and adults do. Jumps over objects. Can copy block letters.	Asks many, many questions. Answers simple questions. "How?" and "why?" are frequent. Word order can be confused, such as "I hurt my knee, and I fell off my bike."
60 (5 years)	Colors inside the lines. Draws pictures that can be recognized. Prints simple words, such as "cat" or his or her own name. Can dress without help.	Plays games that have rules. Knows his or her own right hand and left hand. Talks about feelings. Understands "before" and "after." Can follow three-step commands, such as "Go to the bathroom, put your clothes in the hamper, and brush your teeth." Word order is usually correct, such as "I fell off my bike and hurt my knee."

Your son is rapidly becoming that rough-and-tumble boy who loves to toddle along behind Daddy wherever you go.

Between the ages of 1 and 5, your child will become, to a great extent, the person he or she will be as an adult.

Your child's likes and dislikes, passions, sense of self-worth, capacity to relate to other people, even your child's ability to delay gratification and work hard for what he or she wants, all are shaped during these years.

Your mission, should you choose to accept it—just kidding here, Buddy, you accepted it a long time ago—is continuing to provide all the love, all the support, and protection so necessary to help your child stay physically healthy, develop good emotional health, learn how to make good decisions about his or her own behavior, and develop strong language skills.

From 1 to 5: What Develops?

A great deal happens during the toddler (ages 1 to 3) and preschool (ages 3 to 5) years. At the start of the toddler stage, your child will have just begun taking the first tentative steps. He or she will still be in diapers, but will probably be drinking from a cup, although at this age drinking from a cup is a toddler's version of the *Poseidon Adventure*—upside down and wet!

By the time you and your son or daughter get to the end of the preschool years, diapers are but a distant memory and your baby will have become a little person going off to school.

As your child moves through the toddler years and into being a preschooler, you require a broad set of fatherhood skills. This is your how-to manual.

Choosing a toddler car seat

The National Safe Kids Campaign offers these tips for choosing a car seat for your child:

☛ **Purchase a safety seat appropriate for the child's weight and age.** The manufacturer's instructions list the exact age and size range of each seat. In general, infant-only seats are for children up to 20 pounds and 12 months old. The same is true for convertible seats when they are being used for infants. Infant seats always should face rearward. Forward-facing car seats, including convertibles, are for children 20 to 40 pounds and between the ages of 12 months and 4 years old. Booster seats are for children who weigh 40 to 60 pounds and are from 4 to 8 years old.

☛ **Look for the right label.** The seat should have a certification label that shows it meets or exceeds Federal Motor Vehicle Safety Standard 213.

☛ **Go for a test drive.** Make sure the seat is compatible with your car and comfortable for your child. If the store allows it, test the seat in your car with your child before buying it.

☛ **Make sure the seat is properly installed in your car.** Follow the instructions.

Keeping Your Child Healthy and Safe

By the time your child becomes a toddler, you and your child's pediatrician should have developed a good working relationship. You've seen him or her more than you've seen a good many of your friends. You'll need to continue that close relationship to ensure your child's continuing good health. Two of the most important things you and your child's pediatrician will do is continue to keep your child's immunizations up-to-date and see to your child's routine physical checkups.

For all of your care and concern about your child's physical health, there's no way you can protect him or her

Richard Trzcinski and son Connor, 1997

from life's little emergencies. Short of wrapping a toddler in bubble wrap and encasing all furniture in foam rubber, there's absolutely, positively no way to keep your child free of falls, scrapes, bruises, bumps, and cuts.

There hasn't been a toddler invented who doesn't have a cut, scrape, or bruise somewhere on his or her body most of the time. That's why they're called toddlers; they toddle around, often at high speeds, until they bump into something or fall down. Fortunately, toddlers are still in diapers, which helps cushion their many falls.

––––––––

Bumper toddlers is a fun sport at our house. We've got two, remember? *They love to run in circles, whether it's around the couch in the family room or the circuitous kitchen, dining room, living room route. The sport always ends the same way: They eventually smash into each other at high speeds—wham, crash, cry. We're currently nego-*

tiating with an all-sports cable network for exclusive rights to bumper toddlers. The slogan will be "Bumper Toddlers: More Crashes Than NASCAR." (JR)

––––––––

You may not be able to prevent your toddler from incurring occasional bumps and bruises, but you should do your best to keep your toddler from serious injury.

One of the most important ways to prevent serious childhood injury is to make sure you are using an approved toddler car seat.

As your child moves into the preschool years—and out of a toddler car seat—make sure that your child always buckles up.

Even a short trip to the grocery store can have a disastrous ending if a fender bender sends your child flying into the dashboard. You should never start the car before everyone is strapped securely in their seats.

Fostering Your Child's Emotional Health

What is emotional health and where do I get some? That question seems so complicated it keeps an apparent 1.5 million daytime talk-show hosts gainfully employed. In reality, the answer is pretty simple. Emotional health for a child means feeling:

- loved and love-worthy
- protected
- listened to
- competent

The most important thing you can do to ensure your child develops good emotional health is to show your love for him or her. Do this, and your child will feel valued, loved, and respected. As a bonus, your child will love you back.

As your child enters the toddler years, you need to continue spending time with him or her. Your child needs to know that you think he or she is special. This means inviting your child into your world and becoming a part of his or hers.

How do you do this? Take your child along on errands. Let your child "help" with projects around the house. Doing so will make the errands and projects take longer, but it will also help guarantee an emotionally secure child. Remember, your time is the best gift you will ever give your child.

Join Your Child's World

The "work" of childhood is play. Every day, toddlers and preschoolers are trying to understand things a little bit better than they understood the day before. Play helps children practice how to think in new, flexible ways. Play also helps children develop social skills.

Beginning sometime after turning a year old, children enjoy imaginary play. Children use toys and objects to imagine they are doing something or that something is happening. A child will, for

Let Kids Help
with household chores

Children love to help their dads around the house. Capitalize on this by making sure your child has a set of toy tools, similar to tools you use around the house, with which he or she can help fix things. Here are some examples:

☛ **Painting a room:** When doing the initial brush work, give your child a brush, too. Let him or her paint a wall. Just be sure to smooth out the drips and thick brush strokes your child is sure to leave behind. Once you begin painting with the roller, your child's brush work gets covered up anyway. When your child gets older, you may be able to let him or her try out a roller.

☛ **Plumbing:** Give your child copper or plastic pipe scraps and a pair of toy pliers so he or she can do "plumbing."

☛ **Mowing the lawn:** Ask your son or daughter to help rake, using his or her toy rake.

☛ **Washing the car:** Give your child a beach pail and a small kitchen sponge. Put on your bathing suits and enjoy!

example, pretend he or she is feeding a baby doll with a spoon or that a toy plane is flying the whole family to Gramma's house.

One of the best ways you can help your child's development is to join your child's world of play. Get on the floor and play with your child. Participate in a make-believe tea party or help build a skyscraper to the moon.

The key to playing with kids is to let them set the pace and dictate the action. Play has serious consequences for children. So you need to come up with ways to play with your children:

☛ **Take your toddler's lead.** If your child is pretending a shoe is a phone, you can "call" Gramma on the shoe.

When Daddy has to say good-bye

Many men have to travel as part of their jobs. Here are some tips for making these separations less difficult for your children:

☞ **Prepare your child.** Even infants become anxious when Dad is missing. It's a good idea to give your child an explanation for why you'll be gone a while.

☞ **Reassure your child you will return.** Make sure your child understands your absence is only temporary. One way to do this is to mark a special calendar indicating how long you will be gone and when you will return. Have your wife count the days until your return by putting a sticker or checkmark on the calendar for each day you are gone.

☞ **Tape-record a special message or bedtime story for your child.** Children are tremendously reassured by the sound of their dad's voice. Tape-record yours and let your child listen to it as much as he or she wants during your absence.

☞ **Give your child a transitional object.** Children find it helpful in managing their anxiety about an absent parent to have a special object that reminds them of that parent. This can be as simple as a picture of you and your child doing something together or as elaborate as a whole photo album. Or, it could be a stuffed animal you picked out together. It doesn't matter what it is, as long as it is something special your child can physically hang onto during your absence.

☞ **Phone home regularly.** We know. Business trips are tiring. But both your child and your wife will appreciate the phone call. Spend the time asking about their day, rather than talking about yours.

☞ **Spend special time with your child upon your return.** Don't come home and plop on the couch. Spend it wrestling with your child on the floor or sitting your child on your lap and listening to how his or her days went. Don't forget your wife—or your absence may become permanent!

☞ **If possible, bring a child along with you.** Sometimes it is possible to combine a business trip with pleasure. As all veteran business travelers know, airplane fares that include a Saturday night stay-over are far more inexpensive than airfares during the week. Some businesses will pay for the added expense of a Saturday night stay-over if it results in a substantially cheaper airfare. If so, consider bringing one of your children on a business trip and spend the weekend with him or her. Even if the trip takes you to Gulf Port, Mississippi, instead of Paris, France, your child will be thrilled to be traveling with you and spending time with Dad.

☞ **Play toddler-level football, soccer, baseball, basketball, etc.** This means no rules, just throwing, running, kicking, or tackling.

☞ **Come prepared.** Buy toddler sports equipment: soft, mushy baseballs and footballs; small, plastic basketball hoops.

One final note: Don't leave the mundane tasks of parenting to your wife. Taking your son or daughter to child care or to the doctor are good opportunities for interaction with your child. That time in the car is useful for more than just cranking up those old cassettes your wife can't stand. It's a great opportunity for conversations with your child.

Unfortunately, my work requires that I travel a good deal. *One morning, just before I left on one of my trips, I got the idea to leave a special note in each of my children's lunch boxes. Nothing much was said about the note, so I didn't think it had much effect. The next week I had another trip. After boarding the airplane, I opened my briefcase to find one of my daughters had deposited into my briefcase a hand-drawn picture with the inscription, "I love you, Daddy." I could have flown that day without the benefit of an airplane. (WH)*

Getting Along with Other Children

You want your child to have the chance to develop friendships. Some children develop the ability to make and keep friends easily; others have more difficulty learning this crucial skill. As your child enters the preschool years, you may need to act as a social coach. To know how to help your child develop good social skills, you will first need a quick course on the way children play with other children.

As children develop, they engage in different types of play with other children. One- to 3-year-old children usually play alongside of other children; they don't actually play with other children. This side-by-side play is a natural first step toward getting along with other children.

Three-year-olds will talk with other children and play together in small groups. But 3-year-old children are just learning how to play with other children. Screams of "It's mine!" or "Gimme!" or "You can't play here!" are not unusual.

A 4-year-old child, on the other hand, can be extremely social. The 4-year-old child enjoys playing with one or several other children. Much of their play is "let's pretend": Let's pretend to be truck drivers, football players, monsters, teachers, good guy and bad guy, and so on and so on.

Like everything else in life, developing good social skills requires practice. You can help your child develop good social skills by ensuring he or she has the opportunity to interact with other children. If your child is not in a preschool setting, you may want to consider inviting children from the neighborhood to your house for playtime.

You and parents of children who are the same age may want to form a play group, taking turns bringing the children to each other's houses.

When your child is playing with other children, keep an eye or ear out, but don't rush in to break up arguments. Children need to learn how to negotiate and figure out disagreements. If it looks

John Hamling with daughter Mary Ellen and son James, 1931

as if the children can't seem to figure out a suitable answer or the squabble looks as if it's about to turn into a real fight, then you need to step in. Suggest a solution or direct the children toward another, more tranquil activity.

Learning to Tolerate Frustration

Good emotional health also is reflected in an increasing ability to cope with frustration. No baby has yet been born that can cope with frustration. When babies are frustrated, they cry until someone comes and takes care of their needs. But children need to develop, slowly and over time, the

John Dennis and son Max, 1997

the big girl toilet," I replied. She puzzled at this for a moment, walked over to the bathroom, took down her pants, removed her diaper, jumped up on the toilet, and promptly made "wee wee." From that day forward, she never again needed a diaper. Lesson: Let toilet training wait until your child is ready, interested, and motivated. It will be a lot easier on both of you. (WH)

capacity to inhibit negative impulses and deal with frustration. If a child doesn't learn how to deal with frustration, he or she may have difficulty throughout life.

A good way to help teach frustration tolerance to a toddler or a preschooler is by playing games with them. Some parents believe children always should be allowed to win at games. This is a mistake. Your child needs to learn how to handle frustration, and it's best to learn early. Losing a game of Chutes and Ladders or Candyland to Dad once in a while is a good way for your child to learn how to cope with frustration. So, don't let your child win every game the two of you play. (And remember to be a good sport yourself when you lose.)

Toilet training with my oldest daughter did not go well. *I simply pushed her too quickly and became much too upset at subsequent regressions. Determined not to repeat my mistake (I am, after all, a trained child psychologist), I did not even bring up the subject with my youngest daughter. Finally, at age 2½, my daughter, who desperately wanted to join her big sister at the local preschool, asked, "When can I go to the big girl school?" "When you are no longer using diapers and are using*

Teaching Good Behavior

As we mentioned in the previous chapter, teaching your child good behavior and manners is important for lots of reasons. Children who know how to behave are more likely to do well in school, to get along well with peers, and to develop strong self-esteem. You have to pay even more attention to this important area as your child grows older.

When it comes to teaching your child good behavior, you should have two goals in mind: 1) Your son or daughter should learn what behavior you and your wife expect. 2) Your child should begin to develop the capacity to make good decisions about his or her own behavior.

The two best ways to teach your child good behavior are to show love and set limits. You'll be showing your child he or she is safe and loved, which will allow and encourage him or her to develop self-control.

We've already talked about showing love. By now, you should be doing lots of hugging and lots of saying, "I love you," to your child. That should never stop. Now let's talk about the limits.

Children want and need parents who set limits on behavior. Children need to know their parents will protect them both from mistakes in judgment and from their own impulses. Children are more

A Word about
toilet training

Toilet training can take place as early as 2 years old and as late as 4 years old. It really depends on your child. Most parents want their children to be toilet-trained as early as possible, but it's not something you should try to force on a child. In fact, the best piece of advice about toilet training is: Don't turn it into a fight. You will lose. This is one area where your child has the upper hand. Turning it into a fight will only ensure that toilet training takes longer and is frustrating for you, your wife, and your child.

A few other words of advice:

☛ **Start at the right time.** You should refrain from attempting to toilet-train your child until after he or she is at least 2 years old.

☛ **Use a potty chair.** A potty chair allows your child's feet to touch the ground, which makes them feel more secure while sitting on the potty.

☛ **Treat the potty as something special.** Let your child know that you view sitting on the potty as a sign of being grown up.

☛ **Be patient.** Don't hurry your child. Don't push your child. Don't say, "Come on, come on, let's get going." Treat your child's time sitting on the potty—which can seem endless—as a positive experience, even if your child does nothing while on the potty.

☛ **Reward your child appropriately.** Use only praise and positive reinforcement during toilet training. Never punish a child if he or she fails to use the toilet.

willing to try new things if they know their parents have set limits on how far their explorations can go. Limits help children build self-confidence by slowly but surely helping them be successful in the real world.

Up until about age 1 year, the best technique for handling temper tantrums and other inappropriate behavior is distraction—giving your child another toy, for example, if a sibling has snatched one away. After your child's first birthday, this gets more complicated.

Here are some tips for setting limits and helping your toddler and preschooler develop appropriate behavior:

☛ **Set clear rules and enforce them.** Every family has different rules, although hitting and refusing to follow instructions are behaviors that should not be allowed in any household. You and your wife need to determine what behavior is allowed and what behavior is not allowed. This is an ongoing discussion.

Initially, set a few simple rules and be consistent about enforcing them. Having too many rules to follow can be confusing and frustrating to a toddler. As your child gets older, he or she will be able to understand and tolerate a greater number of rules and more complex ones. The point is to establish early on that there are things called rules and that you are ready and willing to enforce them.

☛ **Be consistent.** If you discipline your child for a behavior one day, discipline him or her for the same behavior the next day. Doing otherwise will be confusing for your child and will only encourage him or her to keep testing the rule to find out how it can be bent.

☛ **Never give in to a tantrum.** Giving in only teaches children that if they scream loud enough or long enough, they will get their way.

☛ **Slowly introduce your child to household chores.** It is important early in a child's life to communicate the message that everyone is expected to contribute to the household.

Obviously, what toddlers can contribute is mostly symbolic and will require a great deal of supervision and help from you.

Teaching your child that everyone—Mom, Dad, the kids—must pitch in around the house and that

Discipline Wars

One of the most common sources of marital arguments is disagreements over discipline. Here are some suggestions for working out these differences:

☞ **Discuss your discipline ideas with each other.** The best way to head off conflict over discipline is to talk about how you want to handle situations before they happen. Work out a discipline strategy beforehand and you'll greatly reduce the likelihood of arguments later on.

☞ **Allow for differences.** You should work at appreciating the different strengths that fathers and mothers bring to the parenting equation. Typically, but certainly not always, fathers are more successful at exerting control over their children's behavior, whereas mothers are more sensitive to the emotional needs of their children. One is not better than the other. Children need both to develop well.

This does not mean fathers should do all the disciplining, nor that mothers should do all the nurturing. But by appreciating the fact that fathers and mothers have different strengths and that children need both, you can work together as a team instead of fighting about who is right.

☞ **Let the first in win.** One surefire strategy for minimizing conflict about discipline is this simple rule: Whoever initiates disciplinary action controls the situation. The role of the other spouse is to back up the disciplinary decision of the first one on the scene. There will be plenty of time later to discuss in private alternative ways of handling the situation.

☞ **Get help when you need it.** If you and your wife find yourselves arguing a lot about discipline, or if one or both of you frequently loses his or her temper when disciplining your child, seek professional help. An outside mediator can help resolve differences and teach you how to avoid becoming angry or upset when disciplining your child.

It doesn't matter what chores you ask your child to do, as long as they are within his or her physical and cognitive capacities to perform.

☞ **Keep anger out of discipline.** It's difficult, but do your best. Discipline is about teaching, not venting your anger.

Don't confuse bad behavior with a bad child. When your child breaks a rule, let him or her know you don't like the behavior. But don't let your child think you don't like him or her. It's the behavior you don't like.

☞ **Don't hit.** We recognize that many parents use spanking as a form of discipline. Unfortunately, this can teach your child to fear you. You want respect. You don't want your child to fear you.

Spanking can also teach your child that hitting is an appropriate way to solve problems. And you certainly don't want to do that. Our best advice is to learn to discipline without hitting.

☞ **Use time-out.** Having your child sit quietly in a designated place as a consequence for poor behavior is known as time-out. When you place your child in a time-out, you should not allow your child to leave the time-out place until after he or she has sat quietly for the specified amount of time.

A good rule of thumb is one minute of quiet time-out per one year of age, up to five minutes. If you wish, you may speak to your child about his or her misbehavior after the time-out, but you should not pay attention to your child by speaking to him or her while he or she is in time-out.

Never, never allow your child to leave time-out while he or she is still kicking, screaming, or other-

no one is entitled to just sit around and be waited on is well worth the effort.

It is best to begin with simple requests, such as helping pick up a few toys or helping hang up a coat or jacket.

Gradually move on to more advanced chores, such as setting the table or helping fold the laundry.

wise throwing a fit. The time-out spot can be any-where you want it to be, as long as you can keep an eye on your child to make sure he or she does not leave time-out before you say so.

Some parents use the bottom stair on a staircase as a time-out spot (usually stairways are conveniently located in the middle of the house).

When you are away from home, any spot that is safe and in viewing distance is OK for you to use as a time-out spot. (If you're at a park or the zoo, for example, you might designate a time-out tree, with the children having to stand or sit next to the trunk of the tree.)

Many parents worry their child will not stay in time-out. Usually, a child will stay in time-out if you direct them in a stern (but calm) voice.

If your child does refuse to stay in time-out, you should consult a more detailed book on the subject or seek professional advice. Just make sure that you never use a locked room or closet as a time-out spot. You should stop using time-out after your child is 10 or 11 years old.

☞ **Praise good behavior.** Let your child know when you like his or her behavior. Praise from a parent is a powerful motivator for a child.

☞ **Combine rules and limit setting with explanations.** Giving explanations for rules helps children internalize them.

When children internalize rules, they will follow the rules even when you are not around, which, after all, is the whole point of teaching them discipline in the first place.

☞ **Be a good model.** One of the best ways to teach your child how to behave is to show him or her the behavior you expect to see.

Children learn much of their behavior by watching their parents. If you are rude to others or curse around the house, you will have a child who is rude to others or uses swear words. On the other hand, if you routinely treat your wife and children with

respect and courtesy, then your children will imitate your behavior and will treat their mother and siblings with respect.

Surviving the Terrible Twos

Around the age of 2 years, "no" will become one of your child's favorite words. Almost everything, it seems, is a fight. "No" is such an important word to 2-year olds, that sometimes they might say "no" or shake their head "no," even when they mean "yes."

Mark Vella and daughter Nola, 1997

Many parents dread this stage. Indeed, one of the most frequently asked questions of child-rearing experts by parents of toddlers is: What can we do to avoid the terrible twos? The answer is very little—and thank goodness. The fact of the matter is that this stage is important in the development of a healthy child. Your child is merely practicing doing things by himself or herself and checking out which behaviors you will allow.

For your child, the terrible twos are about:
- practicing being independent
- learning the limits of that independence
- learning that Mom and Dad will provide protection as the child explores the world
- learning what behaviors Mom and Dad will and won't allow

For you and your wife, the terrible twos are about maintaining your patience under a constant assault of "No," "Me do it," and tantrums.

At this stage in life your child has developed the physical and language skills needed to begin mastering his or her world. Your child is building his or her sense of independence. Your child is also learning the limits of that independence.

At 2, a child is capable of getting into serious danger—dashing into the street, for example. Your child needs to know that you and your wife will keep him or her safe.

Two-year-old children often run away from their parents at the most inopportune times, laughing all the way. During that dash away from Mom or Dad, your child is experiencing both the excitement of being able to run from you and the joy of knowing you will catch him or her before danger strikes.

Your child's growing independence also means testing himself or herself and testing you as well. Your 2-year-old has lots of new abilities, but your child doesn't yet know what he or she is allowed to do with those new abilities. Thus, all the testing, exhibited by the repetition of "no" and the refusing to listen. Your child needs to learn what behaviors you will allow and which you won't allow.

Keep in mind that all of that drive-you-crazy, 2-year-old behavior isn't about purposefully being a brat—at least, not most of the time. It's your child's first experience with that weird dichotomy of being a person: hard-charging independence coupled with scary vulnerability.

Learn to Say
you're sorry

We all slip up at times. Being a parent can be an exhausting job, and sometimes we all lose our temper or say something hurtful to a child. When that happens, the only thing to do is apologize. As soon as things calm down, tell your child you are sorry and you behaved poorly. This teaches your child how to handle mistakes, that relationships take work, and that even fathers are not perfect.

Your child's lucky to have you and your wife to help this whole process go smoothly. Here are a few tips to help see you through:

☛ **Praise the good.** Work at paying attention to and praising your child's good behavior. A good rule of thumb is to work at giving at least twice as many praising statements as critical ones.

☛ **Give choices.** Rather than asking, "Do you want cereal for breakfast?" (to which your 2-year-old will invariably say, "no"), say, "Do you want oatmeal or corn flakes for breakfast?" Don't overwhelm a child with too many choices. "Do you want to wear your red shirt or your white shirt?" is better than, "What do you want to wear today?"

☛ **Pick your fights.** Not every negative behavior needs a response. Sometimes the best response is to ignore the behavior.

☛ **Be consistent.** Don't change rules from one day to the next.

☛ **Look for positive times together.** Try not to let an entire day or evening get defined by your child's negative behavior. Get out of the house and do something your child enjoys, such as taking a trip to the park. You won't be rewarding bad behavior; you'll be creating an opportunity for an enjoyable time together.

☛ Make sure your child gets plenty of rest and food. Here's a simple equation: Tired kids = more tantrums = tired parents. The same goes for hungry kids. So, make sure your child gets plenty of sleep and is well nourished with nutritious snacks.

☛ Take a break. Give yourself and your wife as many breaks as possible. Two-year-olds can be tough. Hire a baby-sitter and go on dates.

A day marked by my (JR's) 2-year-old daughter's incessant whining and screaming (that girl can really scream!) was finally coming to an end. "I can't wait for that girl to go to sleep," my wife said in exasperation as she fixed a plate of Sunday supper for her brother, who was on his way over to our house.

I looked over at Justin, Mylene's twin brother, who was just taking off his diaper in preparation for a bubble bath. "Well, at least Justin has been good all day," I said to my wife. As if on cue, Justin threw his wet diaper at his mother—the diaper landed squarely in the plate of food. Ah, life with 2-year-olds!

Learning to Communicate

We can't say enough about teaching good language skills. A child who shows up the first day of school with well-developed language skills is a child well prepared to succeed in the classroom. Talking to your child, listening to what he or she has to say, and reading to your child are the best ways to help your child prepare for academic success. They also happen to be good ways to show your child you care about him or her.

Conversing with a child isn't always easy. Sometimes they seem to talk in circles or take forever to get a thought out. Other times they speak in rapid-fire sentences, with their words coming out faster than you can listen. Even the best father finds himself tempted to tune out a child at times.

Of course, all of us men are terrific communicators. Our wives will testify to the fact that we can say "Mmm-mmm" or "Uh-huh" and watch television all at the same time. Having conversations with a 2-year-old, on the other hand, can be a bit more challenging.

Mike Rothwell with daughters Olivia and Gretta, 1997

These tips will help you help your toddler build his or her use of language:

☛ Pay attention. Turn off or tune out anything that can get in the way of conversations with your child. In particular, make a point of turning the TV off during family mealtime. In fact, we would argue that a TV has little place in a kitchen. It doesn't puree, slice, dice, or chop.

☛ Expand on what your child says. After your child says, "Daddy eat," respond with "Daddy is eating a sandwich." After your child says, "Doggie sleep," respond with, "Yes, Shep is tired."

☛ Be an echo. Imitate or reflect what your child has just said. When your child says, "Daddy lying down," respond with, "Yes, Daddy is lying down."

(Think to yourself, but don't say, "Yes Daddy is lying down because I'm exhausted from working hard all day at the office, then playing horsey with you, then giving you your bath, but I know there's no way in the world you're going to let me get some rest!")

Dr. Ronald Mells and son Reed, 1995

☛ **Ask questions.** When your child points to an object or holds up a favorite toy, ask, "What's that?"

☛ **Interpret for your child.** When your child names an object incorrectly or can't name it at all, give him or her the right name.

Conversing with a Preschooler

In many ways, conversing with your child as he or she gets older gets easier and easier. But conversations with a preschooler also come with their own kind of challenge.

Your 4- or 5-year-old child can talk at incredible speeds without ever seeming to take a breath. Be prepared for "Why?" "Why is the sky blue?" "Why do we have to eat?" "Why did you and Mommy lock your door?"

The skills you will use in having a conversation with your preschooler are similar to the skills you used in talking with your toddler. The skills are just a little more advanced to keep up with your child's advancing language skills.

The following tips are designed to let your preschooler know you have heard what he or she said and you understand the feelings behind the words. These tips will prompt your child to continue with the conversation:

☛ **Repeat what your child says.** If your son or daughter says, "We had cake at Auntie's today," one way you can respond is by simply saying, "Oh, so you had cake today."

☛ **Reformulate what your child says.** When your child tells you she went to a birthday party, you can respond by saying, "Oh, so you did something special this weekend."

☛ **Ask a question that keeps the conversation going.** "What position does Erin play?"

☛ **Reflect your child's feelings.** Your child says, "The coach put Jennifer in at shortstop today instead of me." You can reflect the feeling behind the statement by saying something like, "I know you like shortstop. I bet that made you feel unhappy."

Taking the time to have conversations with your preschooler is one of life's great pleasures. *One day, my oldest daughter came into my home office to tell me what she had learned that day at preschool. "We learned," she began, "that the same word can mean different things. For example, the word 'may' can be the name of a month or a word like 'may I do something?'" "That's right," I replied. She continued, "And the word 'march,' it can be the name of a month or like someone marching." "That's right," I replied. Suddenly a* *look of utter delight came across her face, reflecting an exciting discovery: "And the word 'april,' it can mean two things, too! Like the name of a month or the name of a person. You know, like April-ham Lincoln!" (WH)*

TV or No TV: That Is the Question

Television can be a fun part of your child's life. Good television brings new experiences into your home. But even the best television, even shows such as *Sesame Street*, cannot take the place of your interacting with and teaching your child.

Language development involves practicing and playing with words and having conversations with other people. A child doesn't do this when he or she is sitting quietly in front of the television, no matter how good the television show is.

Here's what we know about how children are affected by television:

● Heavy television watchers develop language skills more slowly than children who do not watch as much television.

● Children who watch a lot of television, especially action or adventure shows, do not seem to use their imaginations as much.

● Four- and 5-year-old children who watch a lot of action shows may be more aggressive toward other children and get in trouble more often when they get to kindergarten.

● Preschool-age children often do not understand that television is pretend. They may think that there are real people in their television. They also may think it's real when a superhero flies or a person gets killed.

why bother
Reading

Reading to your child is one of the best ways to help prepare your child for school. In fact, research shows that children who are read to by their parents have better developed language skills and higher achievement levels in school than children who are not read to by their parents.

Reading to your son or daughter also makes for enjoyable time together. A bedtime story is a good way to squeeze a little bit of special time with your child out of a busy day. Plus, it's a good way to help your child wind down for bedtime. Here are some tips for reading to your toddler and preschooler:

☛ **Learn to love rhymes.** Toddlers enjoy books that have lots of phrases repeated throughout. Rhyming phrases, such as those found in Dr. Seuss books, are especially good.

☛ **Pick the winners.** Ask a librarian or bookstore clerk about books for children that have won awards.

☛ **Let your child pick the books.** As your child gets older, take him or her to a library or bookstore to select books for the two of you to enjoy together.

☛ **Build your arsenal.** Create a small library of children's books the two of you can turn to for enjoyment.

☛ **See and say.** When you read, point to each work as you say it. This helps your child understand that individual words have meaning.

☛ **Make reading a time for togetherness.** When you sit down to read the paper, suggest that your child grab a book and "read" it, too. Even as toddlers, children love to pretend to read.

If you treat television with common sense when your child is a preschooler, chances are good that your child will treat it with common sense when he or she grows older. Here are some suggestions:

☛ **Be clear about turn-off time.** Let your child know when it's time to turn the television off. Set rules about when and how much television watching is allowed.

☛ **Limit your own television watching.** Parents who watch a lot of television are likely to have children who watch a lot of television.

☛ **Be clear about what's appropriate.** Teach your child that there are children's shows and grown-up shows. Both of you can watch the children's shows. But only you can watch the grown-up shows.

☛ **Watch television with your child.** Explain what actors do and that events on television are pretend. Encourage your child to ask you questions about what he or she sees.

The Last Word: This Child Is Fun!

Not only do we guarantee that by focusing on physical and emotional health, behavior, and language skills that you will be pleased with the person your child becomes, we also guarantee that your toddler or preschooler can be a lot of fun.

The tough thing about being a man is that you don't get to play much any more. The games you love to play (baseball, basketball, soccer) and the hobbies you love (fishing, music) get crowded out by annoying duties such as paying the bills. But now that you are a father, playing your favorite games becomes important once again.

You can help your child learn to love the same activities you love. Simply share your passions. Take the time to teach your child. Structure the activities so your child can participate. Don't push the activity on your child. Invite him or her in with patient, enthusiastic teaching.

The key is to not push. That goes for learning to enjoy music or playing team sports. Your child will let you know when he or she is ready.

Pushing your child into, say, organized baseball too early could well result in your child being completely turned off by the activity. Then you would lose out on having the best playing partner and on a great opportunity to play the games you love while being a great dad.

So enjoy being a dad. It is the most exhilarating, wonderful, rewarding, and exhausting work you will ever do. But take your time at being a dad. Remember to enjoy the moment.

Fatherhood should be approached more like a leisurely stroll than a hundred-yard dash. If you become too busy at work or worried about your career, you will miss out on those magical moments of childhood that give your life its true meaning.

====

One evening, we were driving to my parents' house for the Christmas holidays. *It was a beautiful, starry December night as we drove in relative silence. Suddenly, my oldest daughter, all of 3 years of age, spoke: "Daddy, now I know what I want to be when I grow up." "What's that?" I asked. "When I grow up, I want to be the baby Jesus." After a few more moments, during which my wife and I sat in stunned silence unable to formulate a reply, she added: "Either that or a cheerleader." It's these moments that help get you through the night. (WH)*

====

the many
faces of
fatherhood

**Being a father
is always a joy. But
sometimes it's not easy.
Sometimes there are
special challenges.**

Although this book has been written from the perspective of a married, biological father, we recognize there are other types of fathers, including adoptive fathers, divorced fathers, unwed fathers, stepfathers, and widowed fathers.

Although we believe most of the advice in this book is as relevant to these other types of fathers as it is to married, biological fathers, we understand that fathers who find themselves in different circumstances face unique challenges and, of course, unique joys.

*Allan Shedlin Jr. with daughters
Raya, Christina, and Samantha,
1997*

The purpose of this chapter is to help highlight some of the unique challenges faced by adoptive, divorced, unwed, step-, and widowed fathers and to offer some advice for overcoming these challenges.

The Adoptive Father

Being an adoptive father is like … well, being a father. Everything we've said in this book applies to you. There are, however, a few special things to keep in mind.

First of all, be clear: You are your child's father. Society still communicates some incorrect and harmful messages about adoption. People often speak about a child's

Rick Shultz and daughter Jenna, 1997

"adoptive" parents and "real" parents. This is a ludicrous concept. You and your wife have taken every legal responsibility for your child. You will be up all night when your child is sick.

You will foot the bill for the orthodontist. You will skip important meetings at work to make it to your child's soccer games. You will baby-sit your grandchildren. You and your wife are as real as parents get.

There are myths that surround adoption as well. The most prevalent and harmful is the notion that adoptive children will grow up to have serious emotional difficulties.

Actually, research has shown that children who are adopted grow up to be at least as happy and emotionally healthy as their nonadopted peers.

If you and your wife adopted your child as an infant, any issues related to the adoption will probably wait until your child reaches preschool age, if not later. But if you and your wife have adopted an older child—perhaps a special needs child—the issues are more immediate and more complex.

Here are a few suggestions for handling some of the special issues that come along with adoption:

☛ **Take advantage of post-adoption services.** Practically all adoption agencies offer post-adoption services, ranging from counseling to workshops and support groups. These services are especially helpful—perhaps invaluable—if you've adopted a special needs child.

If you adopted an infant through an agency, you and your wife shouldn't hesitate to go back for advice, even years after the adoption. If you did not adopt through an agency, many adoption agencies still provide post-adoption services.

☛ **Don't make the adoption hush-hush.** Treat the fact that your child is adopted as a regular part of family life. Don't wait until your child reaches a certain age to break the news. The role that adoption played in building your family should be treated just as nonadoptive families treat the role of birth.

Children often are told they "grew in Mommy's tummy." Only as children grow older and ask more complicated questions about conception and birth, do parents introduce more complicated concepts. Adoption should be treated the same way. Your child should hear that he or she was adopted as early as questions about family formation begin to arise: "You were adopted. Mommy and I went to a place where they have special babies for lucky parents who have been especially picked out for them."

As your child gets older, the discussion about adoption will naturally get more in-depth. Show your son or daughter you are comfortable talking about adoption, and he or she will come to you with any questions. Some families even celebrate adoption day—the day the adoption took place—in addition to birthdays.

☛ **Recognize the role your child's birth parents played.** Without them, you wouldn't have your child. To the best of your ability, answer your child's questions about your child's birth parents. If you can't answer the questions because of lack of information, contact the agency where you adopted.

Be as honest as you can about your child's birth parents, but keep in mind your child's developmental age. If difficult circumstances surrounded the decision of your child's birth mother to choose adoption, a 6-year-old child, for example, will not be ready to hear about them. If you're not sure about the appropriate time to bring up these matters, discuss it with your child's pediatrician.

☛ **Use positive language about your child's adoption.** Don't say things like, "Your birth mother gave you up for adoption." No child wants to feel that he or she was given up or given away. Rather, talk about the fact that, "Your birth mother chose adoption for you because she loved you and wanted only the best for you."

The Divorced Father

The hardest part about being a divorced father, especially if you do not have joint or sole custody of your children, is staying in touch with your kids. All too frequently, divorced fathers are treated as if the only thing of value that they have to contribute to their children is money. Far less recognition is given to the importance of fathers remaining an active part of their children's lives following a divorce.

Yet research consistently shows that one of the best predictors of a child's well-being following a divorce is whether or not both parents maintain a strong relationship with the child. Here are some tips for being a good dad despite a divorce, especially if your children are not living with you:

☛ **Phone a lot.** Calling your children almost every day reassures them that, although you no longer live with them, you haven't completely forgotten about them.

Also encourage your children to call you as frequently as they wish. Make sure they have both your home and work phone numbers.

☛ **Write letters.** Phone calls are easier, but letters are more long-lasting. Whenever your child needs a Daddy fix, he or she can get out your letters and read them.

This is one way of staying accessible to your children. You might also want to make audiotapes of yourself reading a bedtime story or just telling your children how much you love them.

☛ **Develop a shared interest.** Sharing a hobby or sports interest helps to solidify a relationship and provides assurances of time spent together.

Even if you are not always doing the activity together, the shared interest gives the two of you something to talk about.

☛ **Keep your commitments.** Every child of divorce struggles with whether or not a parent will eventually abandon him or her. Don't give your child reason to believe this will happen by making promises you don't keep. If you say you are going to come by the softball game after school, make sure you do so. Most importantly, make scheduled visitation times the very last thing you cancel.

Todd Minter with step-daughter Danessa and daughter Brandy

☞ **Make your child's presence felt in your home.** Hang photographs of your child in your home. Put his or her drawings on your refrigerator. These gestures help your child understand that even if he or she is are not living with you, you still care.

Seeing those pictures and drawings on your walls also helps prevent your child from feeling like a visitor in your home.

☞ **Keep most visits simple.** Your children need a father, not a special events coordinator. Avoid overscheduling your time together; you don't have to make every weekend like a trip to Disneyland.

A simple walk to the park or reading a book together often has more impact than big production days.

☞ **Continue to act like a dad.** Part of the work of fatherhood is discipline. Children don't like that part, but it is essential to their well-being. Sometimes divorced fathers are so afraid of losing their children's love, they become reluctant to discipline them. But the divorce didn't lessen your child's need for discipline. In fact, it may even have increased it.

☞ **Continue to be an active part of your child's life.** Show your child you are interested in him or her by continuing to go to parent-teacher conferences and showing up for special events.

☞ **Support and honor the mother of your children.** One of the hardest parts about being a divorced dad is having to continue working together with the mother of your children to raise your children well.

You should be aware, however, that continued conflict between a mother and father is the best predictor of poor outcomes for children of divorce.

Learn to keep any lingering angry feelings in check. This is easier said than done, but if you are successful at keeping hostility and conflict between you and your children's mother to an absolute minimum, your children will benefit greatly.

Keeping a good working relationship may also help ensure that your former wife will be supportive of your continuing involvement with the kids.

The Unwed Father

In some ways, the circumstance of the unwed father, especially if the unwed father is not living with the mother of his child, is similar to that of the divorced father. So, many of the suggestions concerning how to stay in touch with one's child in the preceding section are equally relevant to the unwed father.

One important difference, however, is the need for the unwed father to establish legal paternity of the child. When a man and a woman are married at the time of their child's birth, the law assumes the father's paternity. This is not true when the father is not married to the mother at the time of the child's birth. In such cases, paternity must (and should) be established legally.

Contrary to the belief of many unwed fathers, simply being at the hospital at the time of the birth

Make It Legal

There are several good reasons why, if you are an unwed father, you ought to establish paternity:

☞ **Establishing paternity is a necessary first step toward ensuring you have the opportunity to stay involved in your child's life.** If paternity is not established, you have no legal right to a relationship with your child. In other words, without legal paternity, whether or not you can establish and maintain contact with your child is left completely up to your child's mother.

Even if the mother allows such contact for a period of time, without legal paternity having been established, the mother can withdraw her consent at any time and deny you access to your child. Even worse, if the mother dies before you have established paternity, you become a nonentity in the eyes of the law. You would have no say whatsoever as to who your child might live with or how your child should be cared for.

☞ **Establishing paternity provides your child access to a number of important benefits.** By establishing paternity, your child may become eligible to be covered by any health and dental insurance you might have. Your child also becomes eligible to benefit from any retirement or pension plan you might have.

☞ **If you were to die, your child would be eligible for survivor benefits.** Without paternity having been established, your child would have no claim under the law to any survivor benefits under Social Security. Nor would your child be able to benefit from any inheritance. These financial supports only become available to your child if you established paternity before your death.

☞ **Your child will know he or she has a father.** All children deserve to have a loving and involved father.

Far too many children today who are born out of wedlock do not even know who their father is. Many do not even have a father's name on their birth certificate. If you want your child to grow up knowing that he or she has a loving father (and if you would like to help assure that your child knows his or her heritage), you need to establish paternity.

☞ **Establishing paternity when your child is a newborn or infant is easier than waiting until he or she is older.** Many unwed fathers believe paternity is unnecessary because the mother has made a verbal commitment to allow him access to his child. But circumstances change, the mother's feelings toward you may be very different a few years from now, and verbal commitments are not legally binding.

Should the mother of your child change her mind about allowing you to have a relationship with your child, there is nothing you can do about it if you have not established your paternity. So establishing paternity when everyone is on good terms, will prevent the possibility of difficulties later on.

and having your name on the birth certificate are not the equivalent of establishing legal paternity. Only a duly executed legal order to establish paternity is considered to be conclusive evidence of a father's paternity.

Most unwed fathers have a sincere desire to be a part of their children's lives. Yet only about one in three unwed fathers ever establishes legal paternity.

The Stepfather

Perhaps the most ambiguous and confusing of all fatherhood roles is that of stepfather. Even the term stepparent can be confusing. As originally applied in England, it referred to an adult who took over the parenting responsibilities for a child whose biological parent had died. Today the word stepfather is much more frequently used in connection with a remarriage after divorce.

The great difficulty for stepfathers is that immediately upon marriage the man not only becomes a husband but also a father. In stepfamily situations, there is no opportunity for the newlyweds to concentrate upon and solidify their marriage.

Stepfather Marty Norris with Billy and Ashley Rotza, 1997

Complicating the situation further is the fact that there is a biological father who may (or may not) be involved in the children's lives. This naturally introduces a whole set of divided loyalties on the part of the children. Indeed, stepchildren may feel as though they are betraying their biological father should they establish too close a relationship with the stepfather.

If you are a stepfather, here are some suggestions for blending with your new family:

☛ **Don't insist they call you Dad.** Unless they are infants, stepchildren know the difference between a biological father and a stepfather. The children often view the name "Dad" as reserved for the biological father. Don't be offended if this is the case. Things will actually go a lot smoother if you respect the fact that your stepchildren have a biological father and wish to reserve "Dad" for him.

☛ **Establish a relationship first, worry about parenting second.** This advice may seem contradictory with other advice we have given throughout this book. But according to Dr. James H. Bray, Ph.D., associate professor of family medicine at Baylor University College of Medicine in

Houston, functioning as a friend or a kind of camp counselor initially, rather than trying to discipline or control your stepchildren, can help them accept you. Allow your wife to play the disciplinarian for the early part of the remarriage. This will afford you the time to build a relationship with your stepchildren.

☛ **Don't insist your children be physically affectionate with you.** Like a fathers, stepfathers naturally want to express affection by hugging and kissing their children. However, stepchildren—and especially stepdaughters—frequently feel uncomfortable with such displays of physical affection from stepfathers. It is better to concentrate on using praise and compliments as a means to communicate your affection for your stepchildren.

Do be open to displays of physical affection from your stepchildren, however. If you are lucky enough to be the recipient of a hug, by all means go ahead and return it.

☛ **Support your stepchildren's continued relationship with their biological father.** Research consistently shows that children do best following a divorce when they continue to have a relationship with their biological mother and biological father.

One of the most difficult requirements of stepfathering is to take this research to heart and not only allow, but actively encourage, a close relationship between your stepchildren and their biological father. So it behooves you to do everything you can to make this happen. Remember, we never said this parenting gig would be easy.

☛ **Communicate, communicate, communicate with your wife.** Children are stressful on a relationship. That's why in most cases we're allowed to acquire them only one at a time (JR was just lucky). When a stepfamily is formed, suddenly there may be a number of "new" children. This is hard on the marital relationship. In fact, remarriages are quicker to break up than first marriages. The best way for preventing this is to work especially hard at keeping the lines of communication open between you and your wife.

☛ **Expect the adjustment period to take a lot of time.** Research by Mavis Heatherington, Ph.D., professor of psychology at the University of Virginia in Charlottesville, indicates that it often takes from five to seven years after remarriage to adjust to a new stepparent and changes in household rules and chores.

This is much longer than most stepparents expect it to take. Don't get too discouraged by the inevitable ups and downs of stepfathering. When it comes to being a stepfather, patience is definitely a virtue, as is keeping a sense of humor.

The Widowed Father

One can think of few more tragic events in a man's life than to lose his wife due to death. Fortunately, medical advances make this a far less likely possibility than was the case just a century ago when women rather routinely died during or shortly after childbirth. In fact, up until the 20th century, the single most common cause of single parenthood was death of a spouse. Today, it is a distant third behind divorce and bearing a child out of wedlock.

As tragic as the death of a parent is, children who experience the death of a parent do about as well in the longrun as do children who grow up in an intact, two-parent family. There are several reasons.

First, there is a finality to death that is not the case in other forms of single parenting. Although the child yearns for the return of the deceased parent, in contrast to divorce or other forms of parental separation, he or she knows this is not possible. This reality helps the child grieve and move on.

Second, the child typically does not blame himself or herself for the death of the parent. In the case of divorce, it is fairly typical for a child to blame himself or herself, however irrationally, for the separation of the parents.

A child whose parent has died is more likely to understand that the parent's death was nobody's fault. Thus, as difficult as grief is, it is not usually compounded by feelings of guilt.

Finally, the surviving parent typically keeps the memory of the deceased parent alive in the home. Pictures of the deceased parent frequently stay on the walls and the dressers. Relationships with the deceased parent's family are maintained. The surviving parent also typically evokes the memory of the deceased parent in meaningful ways, saying, for example, "Your mother would be so proud of you if she were here today."

Having said all that, there's still no getting away from the fact that being a widowed father is difficult. Not only do you have to cope with your own emotions over the death of your wife, but you have to help your child cope with his or hers as well. Even if your child was an infant at the time of your wife's death, your child will eventually ask about her and will probably continue to ask about her periodically. This will bring up, over and over again, your own feelings of loss.

If you're a widowed father, here's some advice:

☛ **Take comfort in the fact your children will do well despite the loss of their mother.** As difficult as the death of your wife has been on you and your children, they are still likely to have happy, healthy lives.

Recommended
reading

There are several good books that can help you and your children cope with the loss of their mother. These include:

Lifetimes, by Bryan Mellonie and Robert Ingpen, explains how death is a natural part of everyone's life cycle.

I Heard Your Mommy Died, by Mark Scrivani, helps children with the grieving process by letting them know it's OK to feel sad after a parent dies.

The Fall of Freddie the Leaf, by Leo Buscaglia, uses the example of a leaf experiencing the change of seasons to explain that death is always with us and a natural part of life.

☛ **Give your children time to grieve.** Recognize that for all of us, including children, grieving is a process, not a moment. Frequently, this process begins with denial.

Your child may even insist his or her mom is going to be coming home soon. Denial typically transforms into depression, then into anger, and finally into acceptance. Give your child time to go through this process. (Give yourself time to go through this process, too.) Don't try to hurry it.

☛ **Keep the memory of your wife alive.** Don't be afraid to talk about your wife to your children. In fact, talking about their mother will be helpful to them.

Reminisce together. Look at family photos that include her. Tell your children stories about their mother. Remind your children how much their mom loved them.

☛ **Accept help from others.** Don't try to tough it out alone. Everyone needs help parenting, especially widowed fathers. Accept offers of help from relatives, friends, and neighbors.

☛ **Don't withdraw from social contact.** Of all the problems encountered by the widowed father, perhaps the most difficult is loneliness.

It is, therefore, important that you take affirmative steps to reach out to others and establish or re-establish social relationships outside the home. Withdrawal from social contact may temporarily numb the pain of loss, but in the long run it is self-defeating. Give yourself permission to enjoy life again. Remember: Being happy is not a betrayal of your wife's memory.

For Mom's Eyes Only

You bought this book for your husband, not yourself. So why did we include this chapter just for you? Look at it this way. If your husband gave you this chapter, it means he's actually reading this book. So this chapter is kind of a test. If he gives it to you, he passed! What a guy!

You sure know how to pick 'em! But we had another purpose in mind as well. This chapter is also intended to help you help your hubby along on his quest to becoming a great dad. We'll begin by exploring several myths about parenting.

Myth No. 1: Men and women should parent exactly the same.

In case you haven't noticed, men and women are different. They look different, they think different, and they act different.

Someone even became very famous (and very, very rich!) by making the observation that the sexes would get along a lot better once we all realize that men are from Mars and women are from Venus. Given this fact of life, there is no reason at all to believe that men and women shouldn't parent differently either.

In fact, men and women do parent differently. From the beginning of a child's life, fathers tend to be more physical in their interactions with kids, while moms are more verbal. This is why you like to sing to your baby, while your hubby can't seem to resist the temptation to pick your baby up and swing the little one around the room like a sack of potatoes. It also explains why you believe the 10 minutes before naptime is for quietly reading a bedtime story to your child, while your husband insists that it's the ideal time to teach your child the fine art of sumo wrestling.

Fathers also tend to be more encouraging of independence and risk-taking, whereas mothers tend to urge caution and emphasize safety. This is why at any playground, you will see the fathers, from 20 yards away, urging their 3-year-olds to climb "all the way to the top" of the jungle gym, while the mothers stand nervously underneath their climbing toddlers ready to catch them should they fall, all the time berating the father for letting their child climb so high.

And fathers tend to be stronger disciplinarian figures with their children, whereas mothers tend to be seen as more nurturing. This is why the statement, "Wait until your father comes home," strikes terror into the hearts of most little ones, while children tend to shout "Mommy" when they are scared.

It would, of course, be absurd for us to suggest that every mom and dad conforms to these stereotypes. Of course, there are some moms who like to wrestle with their kids, and some dads who love to read bedtime stories. And many moms are great disciplinarians as well as strong nurturing figures.

We are talking averages here, not absolutes. And on average, men do parent differently than moms do, and in the ways we just described.

Why do we bring all this up? One way that women can unintentionally discourage their husbands from being involved dads is by insisting that their husbands parent the same way as they do. "You're not doing it right" is one of the fastest ways of turning a father off to active parenting.

Of course, husbands are perfectly capable of making the same mistake. The point is that both of you need to understand that, while each of you may parent a bit differently, it is the combination of what a mom and a dad bring to the parenting equation that will ensure that your child grows up healthy, happy, and secure.

Learn this truth, and it will save both of you a lot of arguments over who is "right."

===============

While observing my husband parent our children, I, like many women, have had to learn the fine art of tongue biting. When our first born was a toddler, my husband and I would trade off dinner feedings. His favorite method was to spoon strained carrots and oatmeal into the mouth of our finicky two-year-old while propping her up in front of the television, thereby providing a distraction for her and a source of entertainment for him.

My maternal instinct told me this method was wrong, and would surely lead to an eating disorder of some type, or at least a craving for TV dinners. The right method, of course, was to pretend the spoon and all of its gooey contents was an airplane, locomotive, or some other form of transportation. Never mind that my method invariably led to our daughter's Dr. Denton's being completely covered with clumps of aborted landings while his feedings were much less messy—I was the mother, and so I knew best.

Twelve years later, my daughter shows no particular craving for TV dinners. And all that goo on her Dr. Denton's didn't seem to have any longlasting negative effects either. All of which has led me to conclude that maybe her father and I were both correct. In fact, that's the way it's likely to be throughout this parenting thing. While I have not always agreed with his methods, I can't complain about the results. (CH, wife of WH)

===============

Myth No. 2: The experience of pregnancy should be the same for you and your husband.

You probably discovered this way back during the early days of your pregnancy. When you were delighting in the wondrous joy of learning you were pregnant, your husband was preoccupied with finding the misplaced TV remote control.

When you felt your baby kick for the first time, your husband probably said something like, "That's nice," and then rolled over and went back to sleep. It's a wonder that any marriages make it past the second trimester.

But don't be too hard on the guy. He can't help it. The fact is that pregnancy is less real for men than it is for women.

After all, we men will never be able to experience what it's like to harbor inside of us another living human being for nine months. Nor will we ever be able to know what it's like to have our bodies change so drastically in the process. (And a good thing, too! Given that men tend to turn into big babies whenever we get so much as a paper cut on one of our fingers, imagine how we would act if our stomachs ballooned out into the size of an over-inflated basketball!)

Some "experts" actually advocate that men should walk around with a pillow stuffed under their shirt to better share in the pregnancy experience. We think this is terrible—and ridiculous—advice. There is a much better way to help your husband tune in to the pregnancy: Insist he join you for the ultrasound.

Research shows that fathers who view the ultrasound of their children bond more effectively with their children compared to those who do not.

The experience of actually seeing his developing child makes the child's presence much more real for him. He will, of course, be most intensely interested in finding out whether the baby is a boy or a girl. But that doesn't matter.

What matters is that the baby will now be a real person, someone he will start to talk to at night and pat gently before he goes to sleep.

Just don't let your husband go completely crazy fixing up a "boy's" room or a "girl's" room based upon what shows up in your first ultrasound. Ultrasounds are notoriously unreliable for determining a baby's sex, even with a doctor's expert eye to help. Of course, telling him this probably won't stop him, but it's worth a try.

Myth No. 3: The experience of parenting should be the same for you and your husband.

If you thought your husband was an inconsiderate moron during the pregnancy, things get even worse after the baby is born.

Here you have this marvelous, beautiful, brand-new human being to care for, and all your husband ever seems to be thinking about is how to pay all the bills.

You're enmeshed in this intense bonding thing, and all he seems to want to know is when you're going to be ready to begin having sex again. So if by some miracle your marriage lasted the full nine months of the pregnancy, it's really on shaky ground now!

We will give you the same advice we gave your husband earlier in the book. To prevent these differences from threatening your marriage, you should concentrate on what you do have in common and not what you don't.

So talk about how much each of you loves your new baby. Work at creating new family traditions for your brand-new family. And communicate, communicate, communicate.

Don't let little resentments build. And if you find you are arguing much of the time, it may be time to seek professional help.

Myth No. 4: Mothers take more naturally to parenting than fathers do.

This myth may be the one most responsible for driving men out of daddy-dom. Although research shows that fathers are as capable of nurturing and intensely bonding with their children as mothers, many fathers resist becoming actively involved in the life of newborns and infants because they think that "Mom knows best."

Sometimes moms subtly reinforce this myth because it allows them to be in command when it comes to the kids—sort of a "glass ceiling" for fathers. Some mothers justify this by saying it is more efficient to have one person in control, doing things one way, than it is to work at sharing child care duties.

In the long run, this tendency to take over is self-defeating, for it tends to drive dads away so that when they are needed, they aren't there or haven't learned how to be of help.

The key is to recognize your own, completely natural, desire to want to be in control when it comes to your baby. You can start by fighting the urge to define this as your baby—and reminding yourself of just how much better off the baby will be if his or her father is actively involved. Deep down you know that.

Myth No. 5: Household duties should be shared 50–50.

What? This is a myth? Yes. In fact, it is one of the most destructive myths of all.

We will repeat here a bit of advice we shared with your husband earlier in this book. According to one of the wisest persons we know (a certain Grandma Impi, to be exact), insisting that everything be shared 50–50 is a sure sign that there's trouble brewing just ahead. That's because if suddenly someone believes they are doing 51 percent of the work, they feel slighted and used.

What really matters is not that husband and wife each vacuums exactly 50 percent of the house or washes exactly 50 percent of the dishes; but that each is seen by the other as contributing significantly to the care and upkeep of both the baby and the home.

The problem is that men and women tend to view the value of household chores differently. For example, does 60 minutes of mowing the lawn equal 60 minutes of washing the kitchen floor?

What about auto repair? Is that as important as diaper duty? And how much should working outside the home for a paycheck count? Obviously, there are no right answers to any of these questions. These are issues to be resolved by every couple.

The key to marital happiness is to avoid approaching each day as if it were a test of the other person's good intentions.

One's contribution to the family and the household is not measured daily, but over the long haul. Ultimately, the value of the relationship is found in its flexibility—the willingness of each partner to contribute, even sacrifice, when necessary—and not in some rigid adherence to or search for a magic 50-50 formula.

Help for Fathers

Here are some things that you can do to help your husband be a committed, responsible and engaged father:

☛ **Encourage your husband to parent your child right from the beginning.** Nothing builds confidence like practice. So ask your husband to do things like changing your baby's diapers, burping your baby after a feeding, and dressing your baby. And don't accept "I don't know how," as an excuse. He knows; he's just being a guy.

☛ **Don't "rescue" your husband** if his efforts to parent your child are not immediately successful. When you do ask your husband to take care of your baby, don't jump in too quickly if he doesn't do it exactly like you would.

There are many different ways to hold, burp and soothe a baby. You need to be patient and let your husband discover what works best for him.

☛ **Encourage your husband to become a part of your child's bedtime routine.** One of the most effective and rewarding bonding times is bedtime, so encourage him to spend time helping the little one get ready for bed. And resist the urge to tell him he's "doing it wrong," when you hear the sound of jumping on the bed instead of Dr. Suess.

☛ **Encourage your husband to go with you to your child's doctor's appointments.** By talking with your child's doctor, your husband will learn a great deal about taking care of babies. This will help to build his confidence.

☛ **Support your husband's different way of parenting—in fact, encourage it.** This is especially true for physical play. The more your husband interacts physically with your child, the better off he or she will be. For boys, rough and tumble play is associated with greater self-control. And girls who rough-house with their dads are more self-confident and achieve higher academically compared to those who do not.

☛ **Seek your husband's advice and counsel when it comes to making decisions concerning your child.** Empowerment means sharing decision-making. It also means sometimes giving in and letting him have his way. Nothing will turn off the dad more than asking his advice and never taking it. Who knows; on occasion, he might even be right. You and your husband have embarked on a great journey called parenting. You started out on this journey together, and hopefully you will finish it together.

Along the way, you will experience the inevitable bumps in the road. Always remember that a successful family is defined not by how few bumps they experience, but how they negotiate the rough places. And along the way, be sure to slow down once in a while. The scenery on this road is the best you will ever see.

Index